TO GLENDA GADDIE—

MERRY CHRISTMAS '98

HERE'S HOPING YOU DON'T HAVE TO BURN
ANY MORE RED HATS.

GO BIG RED!

Tom Shatel

Red Zone:

The Greatest Victories in the History of Nebraska Football

by Tom Shatel

Foreword by Tom Osborne

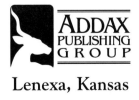

ADDAX
PUBLISHING
G R O U P

Lenexa, Kansas

Bob Snodgrass
Publisher

Mike Babcock
Editor

Darcie Kidson
Publicity

Randy Breeden
Art Direction/Design

Dust jacket design by Jerry Hirt

Photos courtesy of *Omaha World Herald*

Production Assistance: Michelle Zwickle-Washington, Sharon Snodgrass, Gary Carson, Jeremy Styno

Published by Addax Publishing Group, Inc., 8643 Hauser Drive, Suite 235, Lenexa, Kansas 66215

Printed and bound in the United States of America

DISTRIBUTED TO THE TRADE BY ANDREWS MCMEEL, 4520 MAIN STREET, KANSAS CITY, MISSOURI 64111-7701

ISBN: 1-886110-55-7

This book is not an official publication of nor is it endorsed by, the University of Nebraska

Library of Congress Cataloging-in-Publication Data

Shatel, Tom, 1958-
    Red zone : the greatest victories in the history of Nebraska football/by Tom Shatel.
        p.   cm.
    ISBN 1-886110-55-7
                1. Nebraska Cornhuskers (Football team) – History
            2. University of Nebraska – Lincoln – Football – History.
    GV958.U53S52   1998
    796.323'63'09782293—dc21   98-35614
                                                                        CIP

Dedication

To my father, Art, who took me to all the games I wanted to see.

Bob Devaney and the Huskers celebrate another Husker victory.

Red Zone

Table of Contents

Bob Devaney tried to stay out of the way when he stepped down in 1972. But he wanted to congratulate Tom Osborne outside the locker room after Osborne's first victory in 1973.

Red Zone

Acknowledgments

A book is a little like a football team. The author may be the quarterback (does that make the publisher the coach or the general manager?) but he can't do a thing without a good offensive line or sure-handed receivers. Likewise, this book was truly a team effort.

There isn't anyone (outside the South Stadium offices in Lincoln, Neb.) who knows more about Nebraska football than Mike Babcock.

That's why Mike was my first and only choice for editor of "Red Zone." A longtime sports writer in Lincoln who covered the Big Red for years at the *Lincoln Journal-Star*, Mike has written several books on Husker football. I call him the historian of Nebraska football. His expertise in Huskers, history and writing books – and the fact that he covered the majority of the games in this book – all carried this book to the end zone. I've always said writers are the worst editors. But Mike is terrific at both.

Many thanks to my colleagues (and bosses) at the Omaha *World-Herald*, including Publisher John Gottschalk, Executive Editor Larry King, Managing Editor Deanna Sands and last but not least, my sports editor, Steve Sinclair. All supported this book and paved the way for the use of the many fine, unforgettable *World-Herald* photos used in "Red Zone."

There wouldn't be any photos, either, without the help of Ann Walding-Phillips in the *World-Herald's* library. Ann spent hours sifting through the World-Herald's photo archives and came up with some great shots. And thanks, too, to Jeannie Hauser, the *World-Herald's* Chief Librarian, who taught me how to load and use the *World-Herald's* microfilm machine (I think I put everything back in order, Jeannie).

A tip of the sportswriter hat, too, to all the *World-Herald* beat writers whose copy I was priviliged to read through during my research. The prose of men like Wally Provost, Gregg McBride, Conde Sergeant, Tom Ash, Steve Sinclair, Dave Sittler, Mike Kelly, Lee Barfknecht, Eric Olson and Steve Pivovar was an absolute treat to digest. I could literally feel all their toil, sweat and late nights in press boxes while reading their game stories and sidebars. This book, in some way, is dedicated to their efforts.

Thanks to Blair Kerkhoff, a friend at the *Kansas City Star*, who got me into this thing in the first place. Blair, author of "A Century of Jayhawk Triumphs," brought me to Addax Publishing and publisher Bob Snodgrass, who convinced me at breakfast during the Big 12 basketball tournament in Kansas City that this was a worthwhile endeavor. I would like to thank Bob (and for the breakfast, too), Michelle Washington and the crew at Addax for their help, guidance and support. I hope they feel, as I do, that it was indeed worthwhile.

I want to thank my wonderful new wife, Jennifer, who did all the work planning our wedding while I sat in my bunker each day trying to make another Mike Rozier touchdown sound poetic. For her love and support, Jen gets a free copy.

Finally, I would like to thank Tom Osborne, on two fronts. One, for agreeing so quickly and easily to write the "Foreword" to this book. As *World-Herald* sports columnist for seven years, I have given Tom more than one reason to have turned me down. But it speaks to the class of the man, and maybe even to the relationship we were able to have, that he agreed to offer his thoughts. Tom didn't just go through the motions. He submitted, for the first time, I think, his "favorite game" and "best team" in the "Foreword."

Secondly, I would like to thank Tom for, well, winning. Because without him, this book would not have been possible.

Introduction

Good morning. It's Saturday.

And if you are a college football fan – and I assume you are – then you remember how you felt each and every Saturday morning in the autumns of your life. You bounced out of bed a little quicker. Your heart raced a little faster. You couldn't wait to get dressed (in red) and on the road to campus, where you could park and soak up the flavors of the greatest day of the week. And year.

A college football game.

If you are a Nebraska football fan – and I assume you are – then most of your game days have been great ones. Since the Bob Devaney Era began in 1962 (and continued with Tom Osborne in 1973), Nebraska has won over 356 times while losing only 69 games and tieing five. That's a winning percentage of 82. That means, eight out of 10 games, a Husker fan had a chance of walking away a winner.

This book is dedicated to finding the greatest of those games. And the best of those feelings.

What's a great victory? Depends on whom you ask. For former Nebraska coach Tom Osborne, a great game was generally one in which he felt his players performed to or above their abilities. For a sports writer, it's a game with dramatic, big plays and colorful storylines. For a fan, it can be anytime his or her team wins.

But generally, a great victory is much more. It combines all of those necessary ingredients: drama, circumstance, big stakes and emotion.

Often, a great victory is a pleasant surprise that comes without warning. Sure, most all Nebraska fans expect to win every game. But who would have thought the 1994 win at Kansas State, in which walk-on Matt Turman started, would be considered great? Or the 1997 Missouri game, site of the infamous "flea-kicker" catch by freshman Matt Davison?

Sometimes a great victory takes away your breath even when you expect greatness. Anybody remember the 1971 "Game of the Century?"

For most Nebraskans, a great Husker victory was beating the dreaded, smirking Oklahoma Sooners. Nebraska's Big Red has 36 of them. But not all are in here.

A bowl victory is great, but the Huskers have 17 of those. Not all are here.

A victory that clinches a conference title has to be considered great. But in its history, Nebraska has won or shared 41 conference titles. Nope. Not all of those are in here.

When some of those conditions came together, that generally meant you had a great victory. Emotion was a huge factor in deciding the 50. Anytime there was fruit thrown on the Memorial Stadium turf, that usually meant a great win. Games that ended with the Nebraska goal posts taking a dive meant greatness. Victories that prompted normally-sane folks to run around naked at 72nd and Dodge in Omaha also made the list.

If you are not a baby boomer, you probably noticed a few that didn't make the cut.

The list of the 50 greatest Nebraska victories starts in 1962. Obviously, Nebraska was butting helmets on a football field long before then (1890, to be exact). This, no doubt, will be a point of controversy in some corners. Fair enough. However, that is not the purpose of this book. It just worked out that way.

Nebraska has had great coaches and players for decades, men like Jumbo Stiehm and Tom Novak and Bobby Reynolds. Legends all, in their own time. There were wins over Knute Rockne's Notre Dame clubs. And folks who witnessed the 1959 upset of 19th-ranked Oklahoma swear that victory is as great as any.

Well, it is the opinion of this author that, while football or even winning football may not have begun in 1962, the concept of greatness most certainly did. When Bob Devaney arrived on the scene and put his special brand of Irish magic on the product, Nebraska rose to heights never before seen or imagined in the Cornhusker State. Devaney made Nebraska a national player, with the stakes higher than ever. And, as the years passed, the bar kept raising for Nebraska to remain at or near the top. Fair or no, more signficance is tied to more recent decades.

In any case, it's a great topic for a bar debate. Pull up a stool. While I had input from several longtime Nebraska observers, the final list was my call. Feel free to disagree and offer your opinion. But come with evidence.

These 50 great pillars of Nebraska football come in chronological order. Obviously, a case can be made that the 1971 Oklahoma game is the greatest win of all time. But, interestingly, the first selection – Nebraska's 25-13 victory at Michigan in 1962– may have made it all possible. It gave Nebraska players – and fans – the belief that something special was at work here. Devaney knew that. That's why he targeted that game as a must-upset for his men of Corn.

At the end, you'll find the crying-towel section. Two "great losses," were added because you could not have a book on great Nebraska games and leave out this painful pair. In so many ways, they meant as much, or more, for Nebraska even in defeat.

Enjoy. I hope this book will conjure up wonderful, old memories of where you were and how you felt at the time. Or, if you are like me, it will bring to life games and plays and legends I never had the privilege of watching, but enjoyed reading about all the same. Hopefully, it will make you feel like you were there.

It's Saturday morning. Some were better than others.

– Tom Shatel

Introduction

Foreword

By Tom Osborne

In reviewing the 50 most significant games in Nebraska football history, I appreciate that Tom Shatel has chosen a number of the great games in Bob Devaney's career here at Nebraska.

Even though I was not a significant figure on the coaching staff in 1962, I certainly remember the great win at Michigan that signalled to all Nebraskans that Nebraska was a force to be reckoned with in college football after a number of years of disappointing performances. I recall as a graduate assistant coach on that staff, standing in the snow as the team practiced, in December, 1962, and finding out a couple days ahead of time I wasn't going to go with the team to the Gotham Bowl in New York. But I remember it was a great game, but terribly cold. I'm not sure I missed the weather, but I'm sorry I missed the game.

To me, the highlight of Bob's great career was the 38-6 victory over Alabama in the Orange Bowl on Jan. 1, 1972. That capped a perfect 13-0 season and, more importantly, allowed Bob to finally win over his nemesis, Bear Bryant. Bob never won a national coach-of-the-year award, but anyone who knew anything about college football had to concede him that honor that year. He did a remarkable job.

Tom Shatel has also included many of the great games that have been played over the past 25 years during my coaching regime. And there's not a game mentioned that doesn't provide some vivid memories for me.

I'll always remember the first game I coached as a head coach: Sept. 8, 1973, against UCLA. As I was approaching my first game, I know I was curious as to how I would react. Would I feel much different as a head coach than I did as an assistant? To my relief, it was pretty much the same. And I was thankful that the players responded with a good effort to beat UCLA convincingly.

They say that a good start and a good finish is generally a good prescription for any endeavor. I was extremely relieved to get things off to a good start at Nebraska on that September afternoon.

I remember the first win over Oklahoma (17-14 on Nov. 11, 1978) during my coaching tenure was a memorable event. Our players gave a good effort. We knocked the ball loose more times than I can remember on that afternoon. We beat a team that was probably superior to us physically, but no more courageous than Nebraska on that particular afternoon.

We also had memorable wins over Penn State, Florida State and Auburn around 1980 and 1981 that catapulted us to outstanding seasons in 1982 and 1983. I certainly felt we were good enough to win a national championship those two years and I shared the disappointment of many Nebraska fans when we fell short. But at Penn

Red Zone

State (1982) there was a sideline that appeared to be altered. And we went against a Miami team that was very well-prepared in the Orange Bowl the following year.

If I had to pick one game that seemed to lay a lot of ghosts to rest, it had to be the Orange Bowl on Jan. 1, 1995, when we finally beat Miami in Miami (24-17) to win the national championship. That game seemed to symbolize a lot to me and the players. Not only had we beaten a team that was hard for us to beat on several attempts, but it meant I no longer had to answer all the questions about what it would mean to me to win a national championship. The players and their ability to overcome adversity and injuries to Tommie Frazier and Brook Berringer will always be special memories to me.

The win over Florida in the Fiesta Bowl (Jan. 2, 1996) certainly culminated a season marked by controversy. Somewhat overlooked in all that was that that was the best team I've coached. And that was the most difficult year I went through in coaching.

The final game in my coaching career, versus Tennessee, will always be remembered as a game that the players played at a level where they were able to overcome a lack of momentum in the polls – in a way that I had not thought possible. It was very gratifying to see them respond the way they did.

Tom wanted to know if I had a favorite victory in my career. I suppose it would be the 1995 Orange Bowl, probably. Mainly because we finally beat Miami on their home field, where it had been difficult and they had only lost one time in so many years. To come from behind in the fourth quarter, and outlast them and outcondition them, was a real plus.

What is a great victory? I suppose different people have different definitions. I tend to look at how well we played on a given day. That's always a matter of perception. Sometimes a team may have a great name or a great image but you know they aren't very good. People get excited about a win over Notre Dame. But on the other hand, a win over Kansas State might be as good or better. You still appreciate the win over Kansas State because they were good on the day you played them.

I appreciate Tom Shatel's efforts in revisiting so many of the landmark victories in Nebraska football history. I certainly hope the reader finds the following narrative informational as well as inspirational, that the memories would be rekindled of the great players and great moments in Nebraska football history.

The Pre-Devaney Years

Yes, there was life before Bob Devaney.

It was played on a place called Nebraska Field, until 1922, when Memorial Stadium (before the end zone seats, HuskerVision and sky boxes) opened. It was played by men in scarlet red sweaters with a white "N" emblazoned on the front and later with thin white helmets that required no face mask.

They had larger-than-life coaches, men named E.O. "Jumbo" Stiehm and Dana X. Bible. Their first bowl game was in, of all places, the Rose Bowl. They had legends named Guy Chamberlin, Ed Weir, George Sauer, Sam Francis, Tom "Train Wreck" Novak and, of course, Bobby "Mr. Touchdown" Reynolds.

And they won big games.

The first big victory in Nebraska history might have come in 1902 – some 68 years before the first national championship – when the Nebraska Cornhuskers defeated Minnesota, 6-0, in Minneapolis. That Nebraska team, coached by W.C. "Bummy" Booth, did not allow a single point in nine games. And considering that Minnesota was the powerhouse of the midwest in that era, and that Nebraska's record against Minnesota was 4-29-2 when Devaney arrived in 1962, it was a huge win. Big enough to influence the University of Nebraska's athletic board to solicit membership in the Western Conference. They were denied.

One could argue that Stiehm (who doubled as the basketball coach), taught Nebraska winning football. Under the intense, hard-nosed Stiehm, Nebraska won or tied Missouri Valley Conference championships in each of his five seasons (1911-15). But his greatest victory might have been in his last season, a 20-19 decision over Notre Dame. The Cornhuskers, led by All-American end Chamberlin, handed the Irish – with an assistant coach named Knute Rockne – their only defeat of the season. Nebraska finished 8-0 and claimed its share of the national championship, a claim endorsed by *Lincoln Star* sports editor Cy Sherman, but not by *USA Today* or ESPN.

Nebraska had the respect of Notre Dame and Rockne in that era. In 1923, the Cornhuskers defeated Rockne's club, which included the famous "Four Horsemen," in the third game ever played in Memorial Stadium. The crowd, listed as 30,000, was so big temporary bleachers had to be used. Fullback Dave Noble, nicknamed "Big Moose," ran 34 yards for a score and caught another to hand the Irish their only loss of that season, 14-7.

It wasn't a victory, but Nebraska's appearance in the 1941 Rose Bowl (a 21-13 loss to Stanford) was victory in itself. It was Nebraska's first bowl game. Coach "Biff" Jones' Cornhuskers, who were chosen to play in the game by Stanford, actually held a 13-7 lead before the Indians, using a T-formation, pulled away in the second half.

The next two decades were drought seasons for Nebraska football, with only three more winning seasons before Devaney's arrival in 1962. But there were games and performances to remember: "Train Wreck" Novak's 17 tackles in a 31-0 loss at Notre Dame in 1947 and Reynolds' reverse-field 33-yard touchdown run in a 40-34 victory over Missouri in 1950.

Perhaps the most incredible, and unexpected, Nebraska victory to that point came on Halloween of 1959. On that day, coach Bill Jennings' Cornhuskers shocked the Big Seven Conference, and the world, with a 25-21 upset of 19th-ranked Oklahoma, which had gone 74 straight conference games without a defeat. The victory, led by quarterback Harry Tolly and punt returns by Pat Fischer, touched off wild celebrations on campus. The goalposts were torn down. Class was called off on Monday. At the time, it was one of those great, inexplicable moments in college football that come along once in a while.

But, very soon, it would become habit around Lincoln.

The Pre-Devaney Years

Bob Devaney Profile

I wish I would have known Bob Devaney.

Oh sure, I met Devaney and talked to him in his office on several occasions from 1991 until his death, in 1997. And everyone who hadn't lived in a cave in western Nebraska knew of Devaney's legacy. From 1962-73, he won Nebraska's first two national championships, eight Big Eight Conference titles, six bowl games and 101 games while losing only 20. As Nebraska's athletic director, he raised money and twisted arms to rebuild NU's aging facilities. He convinced the state legislature to use a cigarette tax to build a new sports center, the one which bears his name.

But the things that made Devaney a legend were not merely the victories or the records or the concrete structures. It was the man himself.

But I wish I could have covered some of Devaney's practices, just to hear his old salty voice bellow throughout the autumn air and then hear his quips afterwards. I wish I could have seen that red blazer and red hat in person on a Saturday afternoon. I wish I could have attended a Devaney press conference, just to lay witness to his priceless candor and humor – a lost art in coaching these days. I wish I could have bellied up to the bar next to Devaney, on a road trip or in Lincoln, just to buy him a shot and hear his stories. Oh, the stories.

I wish I would have known Devaney because college football is running out of colorful characters. We need Bob Devaney today, more than ever.

A whole generation of Nebraskans today never knew Devaney. He stopped coaching in 1973. But because of the legend, because of the stories, everyone felt like they knew the man. That was the magic of Bob Devaney.

When he arrived in 1962, he was hardly being hailed as a messiah, even at Nebraska, which had had only three winning seasons since 1940. Devaney came from Wyoming, where he was 35-10-5 in five years. But Devaney was a Michigan native and had learned to coach in Michigan high schools and as an assistant at Michigan State. It was MSU coach Duffy Daughterty who told Devaney to take the job at Nebraska because he'd have a better chance to win the national championship there.

Nebraskans just wanted to win, period. So did Devaney. His formula: use a multiple offense and let big, strong boys up front lead the way. And recruit aggressively, including Nebraska. Devaney was determined not to let talent like Omaha's Gale Sayers, who went to Kansas in 1961, slip away. His motto: "Recruit like hell, then organize."

"I don't expect to win enough games to be put on NCAA probation," Devaney said. "I just want to win enough to warrant an investigation."

His recruiting style was legendary. Devaney turned on the charm as often as possible, especially toward unassuming mothers. According to one story, Devaney beat out Arizona State for tight end Tony Jeter when he sat down at the organ next to Jeter's mother and belted out a song.

"Is it true," Devaney was once asked, "that you have gone so far as to sing hymns with a mother to get her boy to go to Nebraska?"

"Yes, I did that," Devaney said. "The mother came to Nebraska and the boy enrolled at Missouri."

He was a master motivator, in the Bear Bryant and Knute Rockne sense of the word. Former Nebraska Sports Information

Director Don Bryant recalled how Devaney set a tone for the new-look Nebraska moments before the 1962 Gotham Bowl, played against Miami on a cold, chilly December day in Yankee Stadium:

"I'm sorry I got you guys into this thing," Devaney told his team. "It's too damn cold, the field is icy and there won't be any crowd. But it reminds me of those old back-alley fights we used to have when I was a kid up in Michigan. There's nobody there to watch, but the toughest son-of-a-bitch is going to win."

Devaney was as smart as he was tough. He hired good assistants and let them coach. In 1969, after back-to-back seasons of 6-4, and a petition to oust him circulating in Omaha, Devaney let an assistant named Tom Osborne change the offense. That was the catalyst to a national championship era.

I've often wondered if Devaney could have survived in today's instant-gratification, big-business world of college football, where he would have been crucified for letting Johnny Rodgers play after his gas-station incident or drinking in public as often as he did. But my answer is an absolute yes, because Devaney had something that transcended the decades, the same thing that kept him touring the Elks Clubs and small-town byways of Nebraska in his last years to raise money and good will among the Big Red.

Devaney gave Nebraskans a national powerhouse football program, self-esteem and laughter all at once. It was during fund-raising banquets that Devaney used to sing the old Salvation Army song, "Tis' better to give than to receive." Devaney never stopped giving to Nebraska.

"He's a man I would like even if he weren't a coach," former Kansas coach Pepper Rodgers once said.

That, more than anything, is the Devaney legacy.

Bob Devaney, the architect of the greatest program in college football.

Bob Devaney Profile

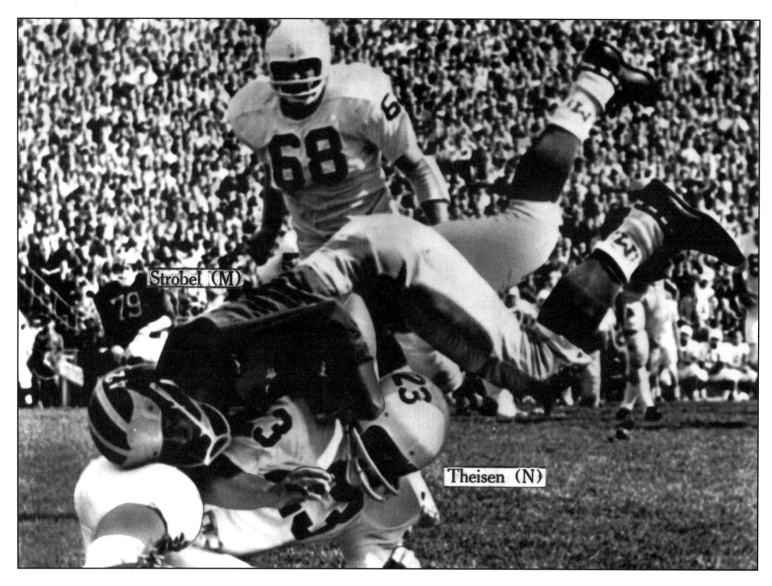

Strobel (M)

Theisen (N)

Nebraska's Dave Theisen cuts down Michigan's Jack Strobel.

Red Zone

Red Zone Game 1

Nebraska 25, Michigan 13
Sept. 29, 1962

ANN ARBOR, Mich. – Lt. R.J. McMeen had been on the Lincoln, Neb. police force for nearly 20 years. But he had never seen anything like this in this quiet, midwestern college town. Nobody quite knew how many people were there. Someone estimated the crowd at 3500. No matter. It was a lot of people to welcome home the Nebraska football team at the Lincoln Municipal Airport.

McMeen and the Lincoln police force were overwhelmed by the Cornhuskers' welcoming committee, almost as overwhelmed as all of Nebraska was over its team's 25-13 upset over Michigan that day. The cars overflowed all available parking lots and were backed up nearly a mile to the Highway 34 junction. If you were a Husker fan you had to be there. This scene alone was one of the biggest events, to date, in Nebraska football history. This was a program that hadn't had a winning record since 1954. A program with only two bowl appearances – both losses in 1941 and 1955 – in its history.

Since then, there have been five national championships and a tradition of winning seasons and major bowl appearances. And it might have started right here.

That was Bob Devaney's logic, anyway. At the time, Devaney was no savior, just a good-looking coach from Wyoming in charge of putting Nebraska on the college football map. Devaney knew of a quick, if not necessarily easy, way to do that: beat Michigan.

The Huskers had opened the Devaney era with a 53-0 beating of South Dakota. But that was South Dakota. Walking into Michigan Stadium and stealing a victory in front of 57,254 fans would be another matter for the Nebraska farm boys.

But Nebraska, enthusiastic because of a new-look, multiple offense, struck first behind quarterback Dennis Claridge, halfback Dennis Stuewe and fullback Bill "Thunder" Thornton. They were a gutsy trio. Claridge led scoring drives of 63, 81, 38 and 75 yards while running for one touchdown. Stuewe, a senior from Hamburg, Minn., led all rushers with 60 yards and scored the first touchdown from 11 yards in the second quarter despite an ankle injury that kept him on the sidelines the entire second half. Thornton, who rushed for 40 yards and threw countless crucial blocks, was an inspiration merely by his presence while erasing questions about an off-season shoulder injury.

It may have been an early defensive stand that got the Huskers going. Midway through the second period, Michigan drove from its 27 to the Nebraska 17, where fullback Bill Dodd missed a field goal. Michigan drove to the NU 42 on its next series, but stalled when tackle Al Fischer and guard John Kirby stopped Wolverines' halfback Dave Raimey a half-yard short of the first down.

The white-clad Huskers took over and went on their first scoring drive.

The Huskers, who led 7-6 at the half, got a break early in the third quarter when Michigan was called for offsides during a Husker punt. Nebraska got the ball back and made it 13-6 in seven plays.

Michigan didn't make it easy. The Big Ten bullies cut the lead to 19-13 with 12 1/2 minutes to play and had the crowd in a frenzy. After Big Bob Brown saved the Huskers by recovering a Thornton fumble on the ensuing kickoff, Claridge led the Huskers downfield with tremendous poise. Despite two offsides penalties on NU, Claridge took the Huskers from their 25 to the Michigan 26 with the big play coming on a 17-yard pass from Claridge to Jim Huge. After a big fourth-down pass to Dick Callahan to the UM 16, Thornton blasted his way for a 16-yard touchdown with seven minutes left. Claridge's extra point attempt failed. But the Huskers held on.

"This is a great win for the kids, the staff and the State of Nebraska," said Nebraska Athletic Director Tippy Dye, the former Ohio State quarterback who hired Devaney, the former Michigan State assistant. "We don't know how good Michigan is but this will do a lot for Nebraska confidence and morale."

The impromptu airport rally proved that, although Devaney warned his players after the game to start thinking about Iowa State. Meanwhile, at the rally, University Vice-Chancellor A.C. Breckenridge warned the crowd, "No one should assume there's magic or a genie coming our way. There's still some strength in the Big Eight. We haven't met any of the Big Eight teams yet."

But now that Devaney had opened the door, everyone else was about to be introduced to Nebraska.

Red Zone

Theisen, No. 23, tries to avoid the Wolverines' Jim Conley (left) and Jim Green.

Red Zone Game 2

Nebraska 36, Miami, Fla., 34 (Gotham Bowl)
Dec. 15, 1962

NEW YORK – Before there was the Orange Bowl, the Fiesta Bowl and the Sugar Bowl, before a Nebraska football fan could count on a New Year's Day trip to somewhere warm most every year and before Husker fans complained about having to play Miami in Miami, there was the Gotham Bowl.

If the Gotham Bowl were alive today, its name would be Independence or Motor City. It was, to say the least, a shoestring operation – one shoestring. The game was played in near anonymity, even in the Big Apple, because of a newspaper strike (no ESPN in those days). Meanwhile, because of an American Football League game between Houston and New York across the river at the Polo Grounds, the Nebraska vs. Miami, Fla., game at Yankee Stadium was set for 11 a.m. It was 20 degrees. The crowd was estimated by the *World-Herald* at 6,166 paid. Go figure.

Meanwhile, the Nebraska team and travel party didn't depart Lincoln until the day before the game – and that wasn't until the Gotham Bowl had placed a check in escrow to cover the expenses.

In all likelihood, however, the Cornhuskers would have played the game for nothing. Back then, even the Gotham Bowl was a thrill for Big Red fans. Because back then, bowl trips for Nebraska came along about as often as 50-degree days in December (this was the school's third bowl, along with the 1941 Rose Bowl and 1955 Orange Bowl).

The game was a very big deal for the Cornhuskers, who wanted to put on a good show, especially before such NU fans as Congressman Ralph Beerman of Dakota City, former Omaha Mayor Johnny Rosenblatt, retired Army Col. Barney Oldfield, a former Lincolnite, and Elmer Dohrmann, an ex-Husker who was an IBM executive in New York.

Both teams put on a show. Though Miami and All-American quarterback George Mira provided the smallish crowd with most of the sizzle – Mira set school records with 24 completions and 321 passing yards – the Cornhuskers provided the steak. Nebraska made the most of its limited opportunities with big plays. Junior halfback Willie Ross scored twice, once on a 92-yard kickoff return. Senior fullback Bill "Thunder" Thornton went out in style with two scores and a two-point conversion. And junior quarterback Dennis Claridge set himself up for a great senior year with a touchdown pass to Mike Eger and a two-point conversion. The Cornhuskers overcame three Miami leads and two deadlocks before Claridge set up the winning touchdown with an interception of Mira. Then Big Bob Brown sealed the victory with an interception at the Miami 43-yard-line with 1:09 left.

Red Zone

Then it was time for the Cornhuskers to enjoy the school's first bowl victory – and the bright lights of New York. They had stayed the night before the game in the Manhattan Hotel, which World-Herald sports editor Wally Provost described as, "a 1400-room ediface in the heart of the theater district."

"We didn't want people back home saying we'd just come to New York to have a good time," Claridge told the World-Herald. "So we came back that second half, improved a heck of a lot. You're darn right we are going to have that good time tonight."

To top off the experience, the Cornhuskers were evicted from their locker room early by the Dallas Cowboys, who were playing the New York Giants the next day in Yankee Stadium and had a workout scheduled. Which was fine with some Cornhuskers.

"All right, boys, the Orange Bowl next year!" NU assistant George Kelly yelled to the Cornhuskers. "The heck with this cold weather."

Years later, when the Tom Osborne teams had to play Miami in the Orange Bowl, this would be an experience to remember.

Bob Devaney admires the Gotham Bowl trophy with Dwain Carlson (center) and Bill "Thunder" Thornton.

Game 2

Four Air Force jets salute the half-mast flag at Memorial Stadium the day after President Kennedy was assassinated. But the Oklahoma-Nebraska game went on.

Red Zone

Red Zone Game 3

Nebraska 29, Oklahoma 20
Nov. 23, 1963

LINCOLN – The country was in mourning. University of Nebraska and Oklahoma officials were in crisis.

Should they play their scheduled game, which was not just any game but the one to decide the Big Eight Conference championship and the representative to the Orange Bowl? Or should they cancel the game and join the rest of the nation in solemn memorial to the death of President John F. Kennedy.

Officials of both schools and the Big Eight had to act fast. Kennedy was killed on Friday morning in Dallas. By late afternoon, the University of Nebraska Board of Regents, Gov. Frank Morrison, coaches Bob Devaney and Bud Wilkinson of Oklahoma, all eight conference faculty representatives and presidents and Big Eight Commissioner Wayne Duke had discussed the issue at length. At 7:30 p.m., the University of Nebraska passed out this announcement:

"The Board of Regents of the University of Nebraska, deeply sorrowful of the death of President Kennedy, believe the people of Nebraska would have the Nebraska-Oklahoma game played as scheduled.

"This will be done."

This was a particularly difficult decision for Nebraska officials, who hadn't won a conference title since it swept the Big Six title in 1940 and went on to the Rose Bowl.

The Huskers had lost to Duke in the 1955 Orange Bowl. But now here was a chance to beat Wilkinson and the mighty Sooner dynasty for a conference title.

The decision turned out to be more difficult than the game. NU led only 3-0 at the half. But the Big Red would dominate on both sides of the ball, rolling up 194 yards while holding Oklahoma to nine first downs and 98 yards.

The dam finally broke in the second half. In what would become a precursor to future Oklahoma-Nebraska bouts, the Sooners literally dropped the ball. As the *World-Herald's* Wally Provost wrote, "First choice of plane seats on the flight to Miami next month probably should go to Nebraska's tenacious ball-hawks...."

Indeed. All four Nebraska scores in the second half were set up by Sooner turnovers, including fumbles recovered by tackle Lloyd Voss and end Chuck Doepke and interceptions by Dave Theisen and Kent McCloughan.

The Huskers were on their way to the Orange Bowl, to meet Auburn. Nebraska fans greeted each score with a barrage of oranges that splattered on the field. After the final gun, many of the 38,362 at Memorial Stadium rushed the field and tore down the goal posts. Another mile-marker in the Devaney Turnaround had been met. The celebration ensued into the night, even as a nation still mourned.

Game 3

Cornhusker back Bob Hohn follows Willie Ross' lead against Auburn in the Orange Bowl.

Red Zone

Red Zone Game 4

Nebraska 13, Auburn 7
Jan. 1, 1964

Miami, Fla. – In two seasons as Nebraska's head coach/savior, Bob Devaney was boldly taking the Cornhuskers where no Cornhusker had gone before. They beat Michigan. They won their first bowl game, the Gotham Bowl. They beat Bud Wilkinson and the Oklahoma machine to win their first conference title in 23 years and play in a New Year's Day Bowl. Now, it was time for the next step.

Win that New Year's Day bowl game.

Win the Orange Bowl.

As was becoming habit, Devaney delivered.

This time, the Huskers had to beat Auburn, from the mighty Southeastern Conference. But if quarterback Dennis Claridge, guard Bob Brown, tackle Monte Kiffin and Co. had learned anything under Devaney, it was how to face – and conquer – new frontiers.

The Huskers did so in dazzling and memorable fashion in this nationally-televised game, before many at home could put their TV trays away. Auburn won the toss and gave Nebraska the option to receive. That was the Tigers' first mistake.

On the second play of the game, from his own 32, the brilliant Claridge angled to his right, cut wide behind his blocks and outran a pack of defenders and broke to the sideline where the 222-pound senior outran the rest of the Tigers en route to an explosive 68-yard touchdown.

"That play is designed for only two or three yards," Claridge told reporters afterward.

The Huskers could add only two field goals and would have to hold on for dear life. This Orange Bowl came down to one last stand: the Nebraska defense vs. Auburn's top gun, All-American quarterback Jimmy Sidle.

Taking over at his 20 with seven minutes, 31 seconds to play, Sidle drove the Tigers downfield, completing three pressure-soaked third-down pass plays. It came down to fourth-and-four at the Cornhuskers' 11 with under two minutes to go. But this time co-captain John Kirby batted down Sidle's attempt to fullback Doc Griffith. Nebraska ball. Claridge downed the ball twice to end the game.

The accomplishment was not lost on the Nebraska locker room, where Gov. Frank Morrison told Devaney, "You have the thanks of the entire State of Nebraska. You represented us in fine fashion and when the going was tough you came across."

Then, as the *World-Herald's* Gregg McBride described it, "The shouting broke loose and the doors opened to the greatest rush of press, radio, TV men, autograph seekers and cheering alumni in Cornhusker history."

Meanwhile, Orange Bowl Commmittee President B. Boyd Benjamin called Nebraska's win "the greatest game in the 30 years of bowl history."

Nebraska fans certainly agreed.

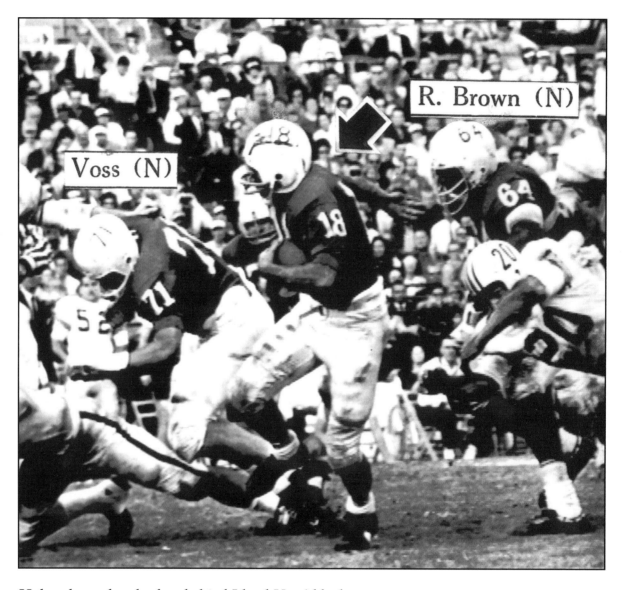

Voss (N)

R. Brown (N)

Hohn almost breaks free behind Lloyd Voss' block ...

... but Auburn's George Rose catches him from behind.

Fearless Frankie Solich hurdles for eight yards of his record-setting 204 against Air Force.

Red Zone

Red Zone Game 5

Nebraska 27, Air Force 17
Sept. 25, 1965

Colorado Springs, Colo. – Long before he took the baton as Nebraska head football coach, Frank Solich was a Nebraska fullback. He was quiet. Diminutive. He only weighed 158 pounds. He was easily lost in the shadows of his linemen or other stars, which, come to think of it, was probably the way Solich preferred it.

But one day "Little Frankie," as he was affectionately called, came bursting out of the shadows.

It was in the shadow of the Rocky Mountains, on a picture-postcard Colorado September afternoon, when Solich had his day in the sun. In a 27-17 victory over the Air Force Academy, the senior fullback rushed for three touchdowns and scribbled his name in the Nebraska record books with a single-game 204 yards rushing. Solich's record, which broke former All-America Bobby Reynolds' 167-yard performance against Minnesota in 1950, stood for 10 years.

Solich's first two touchdowns – 80 yards on the first play of the game and 20 yards late in the first quarter – weren't nearly as momentous as his third. An early Husker rout got a little shaky. A 10-point burst in 54 seconds got the Falcons to within 21-17 and got their boisterous crowd of cadets to dreaming of an upset of the No. 2-ranked Cornhuskers.

But then Solich again was as quick and lethal as a fighter jet. On third-and-two at the Air Force 41, with four minutes left, No. 45 in white and red struck through his left side. It looked as if Solich had been stopped. But no whistles were blown. Solich kept going. All the way to the end zone. That was all the cushion the Big Red would need.

Later, Air Force defenders would complain that they heard a whistle and therefore stopped on the play. Solich said he heard nothing.

Said Solich, "I hit into the left side and was hit. My first thought was to get the first down, but as I spun away from the tackler I felt him loosen his grip. The momentary stop I made was to spin out of the hands of the tackler. The rest of the play was merely racing to the goal line."

The Cornhuskers would race on to their first undefeated regular-season under Bob Devaney (before losing to Alabama in the Orange Bowl). And "Little Frankie" would run on toward bigger and better things.

Game 5

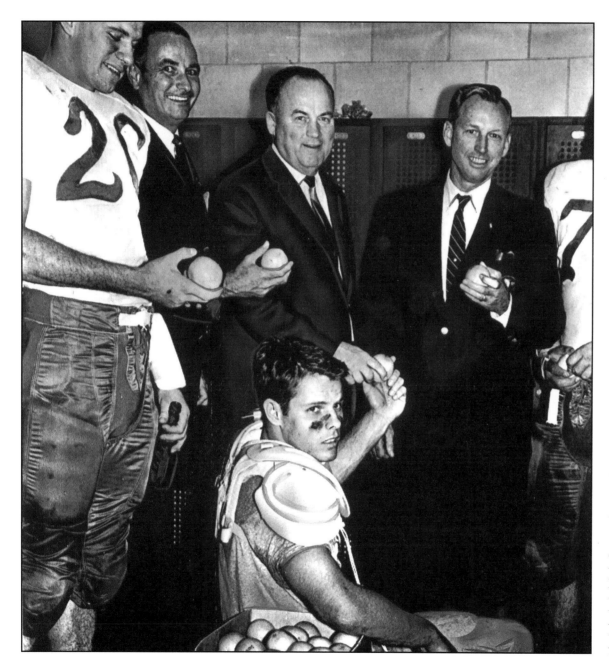

Solich hands Coach Devaney an orange to celebrate the Huskers' victory over Oklahoma State and bid to the Orange Bowl. Nebraska, 9-0, still had to beat Oklahoma the next week for Devaney's first unde-feated regular season.

Red Zone

Red Zone Game 6

Nebraska 21, Oklahoma State 17
Nov. 13, 1965

Stillwater, Okla. – In the end, the Cowboy had become the snorting, cavorting bronco. And the Nebraska Cornhuskers almost got bucked off of their smooth ride to an undefeated regular season and Big Eight championship.

Almost. Walt Garrison, who would go on to become famous as a rodeo star and a fullback with a Dallas Cowboys star on his helmet, took the Cornhuskers for a ride on this murky, blustery late autumn Oklahoma Saturday.

It was called the finest performance by a running back against a Bob Devaney team to date. No. 32 in burnt orange ran and ran and ran and ran. Nineteen times, for 121 yards. But five yards short. The game, and OSU's grand upset plans, ended with Garrison charging, chugging, relentlessly pulling five, six, seven Cornhuskers on his back until they all collapsed at the NU five-yardline as time expired.

Talk about saddle sore. The Cornhuskers were well enough to walk to their locker room afterward and accept a bid to represent the Big Eight in the Orange Bowl. NU, 9-0, had achieved a tie for the title, one they would own outright with a win over Oklahoma the following week. Their opponent in Miami would be Alabama, as soon as Bear Bryant wanted to make the announcement.

But the Cornhuskers had to win the Dust Bowl first. That was no easy task.

NU had faced it all year: everybody was giving their best shot. Oklahoma State, at 1-6, was no different. In fact, the Pokes took the lead, 17-14, with 5:19 to play. Lewis Stadium was exploding in celebration. Here was the upset of the year in college football.

But in a game of guts, the Cornhuskers displayed their own. Nebraska, behind Harry Wilson's running, went 75 yards in 15 plays and regained the lead in the final minute when Pete Tatman crashed three yards for the go-ahead touchdown.

But the anxiety wasn't over. In fact, it was just beginning. The Pokes got the ball back and were able to run five plays, the final coming on an 18-yard run by Garrison, who according to the *World-Herald*, carried Blackshirts Dick Czap, Bill Johnson, Marv Mueller, Larry Wachholtz "and others" until they finally swarmed him down at the five-yardline. The gun then sounded.

There, according to the *World-Herald's* Wally Provost, Garrison knelt and sobbed. Devaney and NU assistant George Kelly hurried onto the field to console Garrison. Nebraska players crowded to shake his hand. But he couldn't talk.

"To see that rugged fellow walk off the field crying was enough to run a chill down your back," Provost wrote.

The relieved Cornhuskers were alive to ride another day.

Game 6

Duda (N)

Cathey (OS)

Randall (OS)

The Huskers' Fred Duda finds himself in the middle of a Cowboy sandwich.

Red Zone

Red Zone Game 7

Nebraska 21, Kansas 17
Oct. 18, 1969

LINCOLN – Oh, sure, there was the "Game of the Century." And you have all the Orange Bowls and wins over Barry Switzer and five national championships. But there are some Husker football fans who would tell you that a four-point victory over Kansas on a wet October Saturday in 1969 was as good as any of them.

And maybe even better.

Let's set the scene. That year, the Huskers were coming off back-to-back 6-4 seasons, which might play in Stillwater or Ames but not in Lincoln. For all he had done to that point, coach Bob Devaney was getting heat. There was a petition drive in Omaha to have him removed.

Meanwhile, the Huskers entered the KU game at 2-2. They hadn't won a Big Eight home game the previous season. Devaney had assembled a young team with names like Tagge, Kinney and Murtaugh who would go on to bring unprecedented greatness to Nebraska. But there are some players on that team who feel the team was fragile enough at that point that a loss to KU might have deeply wounded their spirits. In other words, they might have gone in the tank mentally.

Thank goodness, then, for Mark Geraghty.

The defensive back for Kansas might have changed the course of Nebraska football history with one play.

It happened very late in the day on Oct. 18. The Huskers had blown a 14-0 lead and couldn't hold a 14-14 tie with the Jayhawks, the 1968 Big Eight champ who had a fullback by the name of John Riggins. When KU went up 17-14 with 14:14 to play, it looked like big trouble for Big Red.

Then something magical happened that those in the crowd of 66,667 still talk about years later.

Sophomore quarterback Jerry Tagge, who completed a school record 23 passes (of 36 attempts) for 260 yards, drove the Huskers downfield with time ticking away. Finally, the Huskers had a fourth down-and-16 at their own 31 with 1:58 left. Things looked bleak for Devaney and Co.

Tagge took the snap and was chased back to his 20 before scrambling back and hurling a long pass downfield to tight end Jim McFarland. Oops. The pass was overthrown by about 10 yards. But, magically, incredibly, Geraghty ran into McFarland. Even though the Husker end couldn't have possibly caught the ball, KU was flagged for pass interference. The Hawks' protests cost them 15 more yards and NU was set up first-and-10 at the KU 17.

Four plays later, Jeff Kinney scored to give Nebraska the lead for good with 1:22 left. But the Huskers still had to survive a late scare, when Nebraska chased down KU quarterback Phil Basler at the NU 18 as time expired.

No wonder Nebraska co-captain Dana Stephenson called his team "the luckiest people alive."

McFarland grudingly agreed.

"I don't think I would have caught the pass," McFarland said. "But I don't think they have a gripe. He hit me when the ball was in the air. That's interference.

"If he wouldn't have hit me, that would have been the ball game."

And maybe that young team never would have recovered and Devaney might have been dismissed and the national championship dynasty never would have materialized. Who knows?

Thanks to this miracle victory, Nebraska never had to find out.

Red Zone Game 8

Nebraska 44, Oklahoma 14
Nov. 22, 1969

NORMAN, Okla. – Steve Owens won the Heisman Trophy in 1969. Then again, he only had to face the Nebraska defense once.

Good thing, too, for Owens. The Oklahoma senior halfback had enough problems in his last game, a 44-14 rout by the Cornhuskers on a warm and typically windy day at Owen Field.

A Sooner crowd of 53,500 came out to pay their respects to their legend. Oklahoma, which was 3-2 in fourth place in the Big Eight, was going nowhere. And neither, it turned out, was Owens. For the first time in 19 games, Owens failed to net at least 100 yards rushing (he was held to 71 yards on 21 carries). And for the first time in 16 games, the nation's leading rusher and scorer was held scoreless.

Obviously, the nation's Heisman voters ignored Owens' nightmare finish. Or, maybe they understood that the Blackshirt defense, one of the top units in the nation, was that good. That was Owens' story. And he was sticking to it.

"I can't say too much," said Owens, the last Sooner out of the shower that day. "Nebraska just closed off the inside completely; we got behind and we had to pass. You have to give their defense credit. They did a good job."

There was plenty of incentive for the Blackshirts, led by junior linebacker Jerry Murtaugh, who set a record with 10 tackles. NU entered the day tied with Missouri at 5-1 in the Big Eight and though the Tigers had the tiebreaker with a win over Nebraska, Mizzou was at Kansas that day and you never know in that series. Moreover, Nebraska was playing for the vindication of its coach, Bob Devaney, who had called a 47-0 drubbing to OU the previous year in Lincoln the low point of his career.

So much for the outhouse. Devaney was headed up the elevator after one of his great coaching jobs. The coach had entered the 1969 season juggling two sophomores, Van Brownson and Jerry Tagge, at quarerback. Halfback Joe Orduna, the team leader in 1968, was out for the year with a knee injury. The offensive line had to be rebuilt. It all came to pass, and run, on this wind-swept day, a coming-out party for future Husker greats. Halfback Jeff Kinney, a sophomore from McCook, Neb., scored three touchdowns and passed for another. Brownson directed six TD drives and ran and passed for two scores. The offensive line was dominant.

And the table was now set for an unforgettable run at greatness never before achieved at Nebraska. But on this day, Devaney was neither concerned about vindicating the past nor looking toward the future. He wanted to salute a gutsy NU team that had lost its conference opener to Mizzou and never slipped again.

Murtaugh (N)

Jarmon (N)

Owens (OU)

81

81

FUMBLE

Geddes (N)

"We've had some real fine people play for us at Nebraska, but these guys have overcome the greatest handicap (to win a title) as any I've ever coached," Devaney said. "This very well could be the best football team we've had."

This day was only a preview. History shows the best was yet to come.

Oklahoma great Steve Owens still won the Heisman Trophy in 1969 despite this rough afternoon, a 44-14 loss to Nebraska, in which Owens was hounded all day by Huskers like Ken Geddes and Jerry Murtaugh.

Red Zone

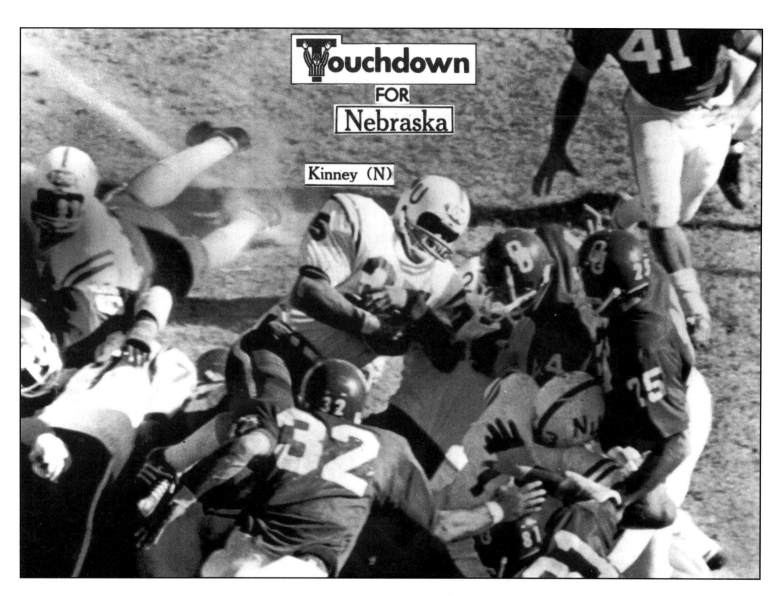

Touchdown FOR Nebraska

Kinney (N)

Nebraska's Jeff Kinney in a familiar pose: bulling toward the goal-line.

Bob Devaney addresses the troops on the eve of what would be an historic night.

Red Zone

Red Zone Game 9

Nebraska 17, LSU 12
Jan. 1, 1971

MIAMI, Fla. – National championship. That's the standard now of Nebraska football, the starting point each and every August. Once upon a time, those were actually foreign words to Nebraska football fans. Beating Oklahoma, winning Big Eight titles and going to bowl games were on each Cornhusker fan's to-do list.

But all that changed on a magical New Year's Day night in southern Florida.

Nobody knew that Big Red football would be transformed, beamed up, to a whole new level that Orange Bowl night against LSU like something on "Star Trek." Oh sure, coach Bob Devaney had taken the Nebraska job in 1962 in part because his former Michigan State mentor, Duffy Daughtery, had told him he could "win a national championship at Nebraska." And even Jerry Murtaugh, one of the all-time great Nebraska linebackers and a senior in 1970, had predicted before that season the Huskers would win the national championship."

Who knew? The Huskers returned experience and dangerous skill-position threats on offense, but only three veterans returned on defense. And when the Huskers let USC come back to tie them, 21-21, in the second game, a national title seemed farther away. But there they stood, 10-0-1, warming up on the Orange Bowl turf, with a stunning version of "SportsCenter" being relayed by teammates.

No. 1 Texas: Lost to Notre Dame, 24-11, in the Cotton Bowl.

No. 2 Ohio State: Lost to Stanford, 27-17, in the Rose Bowl.

No. 3 Nebraska: A victory over No. 6 LSU away from No.1.

The adrenaline of the sudden carrot stretched before them carried NU to a sudden 10-0 lead in the first 13 minutes of the game. But LSU came back, chipping away with a second-quarter field goal and nine points in the third quarter, including a touchdown pass from quarterback Buddy Lee to sprinter Al Coffee, who got open when Cornhusker defensive back Jim Anderson slipped on the play, the last of the third quarter. Headed to the fourth quarter, LSU suddenly led, 12-10.

But now came a series of poise that would be replayed countless times again the next season and would become the trademark of the Devaney national championship era. When the going got tough, the Huskers got going.

The Cornhuskers, who rushed for 132 yards against a stingy LSU unit that allowed an average of 52.2 yards per game all season, moved under the direction of junior quarterback Jerry Tagge. Mixing his plays between halfbacks Jeff Kinney and Joe Orduna, drove NU 66 yards to the LSU one-yardline. Then came a pose that remains frozen on office walls and taverns across Nebraska to this day: Tagge sneaking over the gold and white wall, using a second effort, with the ball stretched out over the goalline.

With 8:50 left, Nebraska just had to play defense.

The Cornhuskers, led by Murtaugh and sophomore end Willie Harper, shut down LSU and backup quarterback Bert Jones, who was intercepted by linebacker Bob Terrio with 45 seconds to play. The celebration was on.

Well, not quite yet. The Cornhuskers still had to wait word from the two polls, Associated Press and United Press International. Devaney knew Notre Dame coach Ara Parseghian would be claiming his No. 6 (AP) and No. 5-ranked (UPI) Irish had faced a greater challenge in Texas. So, to fire the first campaign salvo, Devaney told reporters, "Even the Pope would have to vote us No. 1."

It never came to that. Nebraska was national champion. The words would quickly become part of the Cornhusker vocabulary. Not to mention cause Devaney a bit of grief from offended catholics.

Nebraska's Johnny Adkins (57) and Willie Harper close in on LSU quarterback Bert Jones.

Red Zone

The smiles said it all after the Orange Bowl victory over LSU: Nebraska was No. 1.

Red Zone Game 10

Nebraska 35, Oklahoma 31
Nov. 25, 1971

NORMAN, Okla. – I remember missing dinner. Thanksgiving dinner. But how could any kid – and self-styled football fan of any age – have missed the game they called "The Game of the Century?"

You didn't eat. Or all mothers were instructed to postpone the creations of the kitchen until after this football feast that was gripping an entire nation was through, to the bone. Bone-crunching No. 1 Nebraska vs. No. 2 Oklahoma's wishbone. On Cold Turkey Day.

There had been great college football games before and certainly, classic matchups and plays and dramas played out since. But, with a year left before the next millenium, there still has not been a game that meant as much or was hyped as much and delivered as much as the "Game of the Century."

This was a drama played out on dual stages. One came before the game. Rarely back then was any college game treated to the hype of a Super Bowl. But that's what this was: a clash of Titans. No. 1 Nebraska and its no-nonsense No. 1-ranked defense against No.2 Oklahoma and its top-ranked offense, the flamboyant wishbone. Both schools were located in the bread-basket Big Eight. Both wore red. Both had fans who worshiped football year-round and had been waiting for this game nearly that long. Both had veteran, senior quarterbacks in NU's Jerry Tagge and OU's Jack Mildren. Both had electrifying

superstars in Johnny Rodgers and Greg Pruitt. Of the 22 all-Big Eight players that season, 17 played in this game.

The game was so big that *Sports Illustrated* previewed it on its cover, showing a Nebraska player (linebacker Bob Terrio) and Oklahoma player (halfback Greg Pruitt) nose-to-nose with the headline "Irrestible Oklahoma meets Immovable Nebraska."

The game was so good it beat the *Sports Illustrated* jinx.

That's what allows the 1971 Nebraska-Oklahoma game to transcend time and legend. The game. It was a great game. It had everything you could dream of: lead changes, big plays, Herculean efforts by All-Americans and a final, dramatic touchdown drive for good measure. Adding to the theatric atmosphere was a dark, gray sky with light rain that fell at all the right times.

It was Nebraska's Rodgers setting the pace, right out of the gate, with a 72-yard twisting, turning, stopping, refueling, jetting punt return for a touchdown in which Johnny R. Superstar looked like a pinball on the Owen Field turf. That came with 11:28 left in the first quarter. The crowd and TV audience was out of breath. It was only 7-0.

And then it all became a blur. A big, red, wonderful blur.

Oklahoma kicked a field goal. Nebraska's powerful halfback, Jeff Kinney, scored on a one-yard plunge. Mildren scored for Oklahoma. Mildren then threw a 24-yard touchdown pass as the Sooners, going to the air to keep NU's Blackshirts on their heels, went up 17-14 at the half.

Kinney scored again. Nebraska led again, 21-17. And Kinney again, from one yard, 28-17. But here came Mildren, on a three-yard touchdown run, with 28 seconds left in the third quarter, to cut it to 28-24. Nebraska, which had only given up 23 first-half points all season, couldn't catch its breath on the sidelines. Here came the Sooners again – passing, for heaven's sakes – with Mildren throwing 17 yards to Harrison, with 7:10 left in the game. Oklahoma, 31-28.

But you knew it wasn't over. You knew, even with your mom yelling at you and your dad that the cranberries were going to the dog if you didn't get to the table soon, that Nebraska wasn't through. And the Cornhuskers weren't. Tagge, starting on his 26, later said, "Nobody said a word in the huddle but me. We all knew what had to be done."

Nebraska drove 74 yards, in about five minutes. One of the great plays lost in the drive was a freelance route run by Rodgers on a huge third-and-eight that went for a 12-yard reception. But the signature image of the classic drive was Kinney, his white jersey in tatters, bulling across the goal line for his 174th yard on his 29th

carry. Nebraska was ahead, 35-31. There was 1:38 still left. But it was finally over.

Dinner?

No. I grabbed my coat and football and ran outside. I was going to be Jeff Kinney for a while. Great games will do that to you.

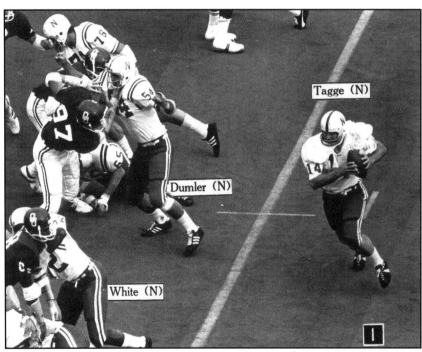

Jerry Tagge, one of the many heroes of the "Game of the Century," follows the blocks of Doug Dumler and Daryl White.

Classic Rich Glover. Here, he snags Alabama running back Johnny Musso in the 1972 Orange Bowl.

Red Zone

Red Zone Game 11

Nebraska 38, Alabama 6 (Orange Bowl)
Jan. 1, 1972

MIAMI, Fla. – This time, Bob Devaney came loaded for Bear.

In two previous games against Bear Bryant and Alabama, the coach of the Big Red came away red-faced. Devaney had lost to Bryant, 39-28 in the 1966 Orange Bowl and a year later, 34-7, in the Sugar Bowl. During a midweek Orange Bowl luncheon, Devaney recalled their previous two meetings and how the Bear would call Devaney and say, "Old friend, let's get together in Miami and have a nice game."

"I fell for it," Devaney said.

But behind the laughter was a Devaney determined to even a score. The Irishman had the team this time – his best team – ranked No. 1. Alabama, unbeaten and untied, had replaced Oklahoma at No. 2. Even the Bear was hyping the game as "just about the biggest college game that's ever been." Maybe for Bama. But Nebraska, which was coming off a gut-wrenching, nerve-checking "Game of the Century," wouldn't take the Bear bait. For good reason.

This wasn't even the Game of the Week.

Nebraska hadn't lost a step since its November date in Norman and it showed. Jerry Tagge, Johnny Rodgers, Rich Glover, Jeff Kinney and Willie Harper were too much for the Tide. And any chance for this to become a game ended with a quick Cornhusker scoring burst in the second quarter.

With Nebraska clinging to a 6-0 lead with seconds left in the first quarter, Rodgers did it again. He returned a Tide punt 77 yards for a touchdown, his fourth of the season and just three yards short of the Orange Bowl record. Then, on the kickoff, NU's Randy Borg slammed into Bama's Steve Williams and jarred the ball loose. Nebraska recovered and, seven plays later, Tagge scored on a fourth-down sneak similar to the one that beat LSU for the national title a year earlier. In the other end zone.

That was more than what the Cornhusker defense would need. The Blackshirts held Alabama, which had averaged 32.9 points per game, to a single touchdown. The bruising Blackshirts forced two fumbles, an interception and humility from the prideful Bear, who called the defeat one of his worst.

"I surely think they are one of the greatest, if not the greatest team, I've ever seen," Bryant told reporters after the game. "They just toyed with us. They just flat whipped our butts in every way known to man. We were never in the game."

Devaney surprised some by calling this his greatest victory. But it should not have been any surprise. Not with a Bear trophy, finally, ready for his wall at home in Lincoln.

"The Oklahoma victory was a very important one for us," Devaney said. "There probably was more excitement in that game because the lead changed several times. But this was for the national championship."

And, for Devaney, much, much more.

There was no stopping Jeff Kinney, or the Huskers, against the Tide to win their second consecutive national championship.

Red Zone

They shall return. Husker captain Jim Anderson poses with Woody Varner, president of the Nebraska systems, with the MacArthur Bowl, the 1972 national championship trophy.

Mike Beran and Jim Branch bring home the 1973 Orange Bowl trophy after Bob Devaney's last game.

Red Zone

Red Zone Game 12

Nebraska 40, Notre Dame 6 (Orange Bowl)
Jan. 1, 1973

MIAMI, Fla. – For the first time in three years, Nebraska was in the Orange Bowl not playing for a national championship. But there was still much to play for.

Bob Devaney, the Bobfather of Nebraska football, the inventor of championship football at Nebraska, was coaching his final game. And the school's first Heisman Trophy winner, Johnny Rodgers, was also taking his final Nebraska bows. It was a melancholy night, but, with the opponent Notre Dame and coach Ara Parseghian, it was also a night to have fun.

And fun the Cornhuskers had.

With nothing at stake except Nebraska pride and Notre Dame humility, Devaney pulled out a surprise for his final act.

He started Rodgers, the wingback and return man supreme, at I-back.

Other than the fact that Rodgers rushed for three touchdowns, caught a 50-yard touchdown pass from quarterback David Humm and threw a 52-yard touchdown bomb to Frosty Anderson, the experiment worked out okay. Oh, yes, and the Cornhuskers crushed the Irish, 40-6.

Rodgers, in one of the great performances in Orange Bowl history, practically upstaged Devaney's finale from the first play. Whether the blocking was that good or the Irish that surprised to see Rodgers line up at I-back no one was sure. But when Rodgers burst for 13 yards off the left side on his first play, it was a preview of a special night. Rodgers (who rushed 15 times for 81 yards) scored four touchdowns (and passed for one) while touching the ball 19 times.

Meanwhile, Devaney opened the whole playbook for this game. The touchdown pass from Rodgers to Anderson, which made it 20-0 in the second quarter, was a play called the "Nebraska Special" that had been in the playbook for years but not used. But they brought it out because, as assistant coach Tom Osborne said, Rodgers "had the best arm on the team outside of the quarterbacks." As *World-Herald* writer Tom Ash described it, "At times, it looked like a sandlot game in which Husker quarterback Dave Humm was drawing plays in the dirt and his team was the big kids playing against their little brothers."

It obviously worked. To painful ends for the Irish, who allowed 560 yards total offense, the most in their rich history. Afterward, someone asked Devaney – who had been criticized for his lack of running game all season – if he had considered using Rodgers at I-back earlier in the season. Devaney admitted he had considered it. But, as heir-to-the-throne Osborne said, the odds were great Rodgers would get banged up at I-back "and he was so important to us that we couldn't afford that."

But Devaney could use Rodgers at his whim in the final game and he used perhaps the most talented Husker in history to make a point: Rodgers deserved the Heisman. There had been a debate over Rodgers by some voters (because of an off-the-field incident early in his career) but after the Orange Bowl Devaney said, "If there is a guy in the country who thinks Johnny Rodgers doesn't deserve the Heisman Trophy, he should quit writing sports or broadcasting or whatever he does."

Devaney was quitting coaching. Osborne was on deck. The most glorious time in Nebraska football history was over – with more glorious days to come.

Red Zone

Tom Osborne Profile

The first time I met Tom Osborne, I was sitting in a hot tub.

It was a Saturday morning in October of 1988, hours before the annual Nebraska flogging of Kansas State. I was in the middle of the Manhattan, Kan., Holidome, letting the bubbles nurse away a Friday night in Aggieville. I worked for the *Kansas City Star* then, covering K-State, and was more than a little shocked to see this tall figure looking down on me from a staircase.

"Hey, Tom, I'm Tom Osborne. Could I have a word with you?"

Osborne, it seemed, had a beef with a story I had done for *The Star*, a story I was ordered to do about a former Nebraska academic advisor who was threatening to sue NU and supposedly divulge the Big Red house secrets. I had talked to two NU athletic officials to get their side of the story. Osborne was busy the day I was there. I didn't want to stay for practice. I left town. And now, weeks later, here was Osborne, looking down upon the writer in the hot tub, chastising me for not talking to him. The least he could do was pass me a towel.

Of course, this was not exactly Woody Hayes doing the scolding. A reprimand by Osborne was like getting chewed out by Ward Cleaver.

What I learned that day was that Osborne was as fair as Beaver's dad, too. He said hoped I'd talk to him next time, smiled and walked away. Now, it was Kansas State's turn.

Osborne has been called many things. Stoic? Of course. Meticulous? Uh, huh. Hard-working? To a fault. Thin-skinned? Oh, yes. But one word fits Osborne like the whistle around his neck: consistent.

Osborne was as consistent off the field as he was on it, and all he did was win 250 games in 25 years, with 25 straight nine-win seasons and bowl appearances.

He always believed in the sledge-hammer offense, whether he had the arms of Dave Humm and Vince Ferragamo or the option-minds of Turner Gill or Tommie Frazier running it. He always ended each practice with a three-mile jog around the stadium or track. He ended each press conference, as quickly as possible, by saying, "Anything else?" He always answered every critic, whether by mail or by visiting a reporter in a hot tub. He loved to get the last word.

Sure, he could coach. He loved to coach. He loved Xs and Os and practices, even – especially – spring practices. Funny, but Osborne was always a better quote, and more at ease, after practice. That was his world, away from media and boosters and recruiting planes. Maybe the whistle was his security blanket.

He would only say something worthwhile when he had something to say, an agenda to meet, an issue upon which to speak out. But Osborne was even consistent about that.

A major part of that consistency was Osborne's courage.

Perhaps nobody in the history of college football showed more.

He went for two points in the 1984 Orange Bowl when one would have given him his first national championship. He brought back Lawrence Phillips late in the 1995 season when he could have been politically-correct and banned the wayward kid from the field. He got involved in his players' legal matters when other coaches wouldn't have touched them with a ten-foot pole. He retired after the 1997 season, with still so much desire inside to coach, to spend time with a family that had missed him so much for years.

Osborne did them because he thought they were the right things to do. Society and Osborne often had different definitions of what was right. But Osborne never wavered, not even when he knew that his actions, particularly in the Phillips case, might label and define his career.

I was out of the hot tub, but not necessarily the hot water, in 1995. I had written a column critizing Osborne's decision with Phillips. I understood why he did it – he was trying to be fair, to help the kid – but we disagreed on the method. I probably heard from the entire state of Nebraska. But never once from Osborne. Why?

Years later, in the early summer of 1998, I had to know. After we had sat down to discuss his "Foreword" of the "Red Zone," I finally said, "Tom, I appreciate the fact that you still treated me with the same courtesy and

respect after that column. Was it hard?"

Osborne went on to tell the Phillips tale again, of how disappointed he was in how Phillips has turned out, and how my being around the program and getting his side of the story was all he could ask of me.

And so the man I had been so critical (and praising, in other times) of was helping me in my first book venture? He was just being fair.

Consistent. That's how I'll always remember Tom Osborne.

Bahe (N) Damkroger (N) Goeller (N)

Longwell (N)

A classic Tom Osborne play in the new coach's first game: fullback Maury Damkroger rambles up the middle against UCLA.

Red Zone Game 13

Nebraska 40, UCLA 13
Sept. 8, 1973

LINCOLN – On the morning of Sept. 8, 1973, the state of Nebraska woke up with a giant butterfly in its collective stomach.

As Cornhusker fans prepared for the drive down I-80 to Memorial Stadium or warmed up their TV sets for the season-opener against UCLA, nobody could have known that this was the beginning of a new era. An era that would last 25 seasons and reap three national championships, several Big Eight championships and major bowl appearances in almost every year. No, all anyone in red knew that day was that Bob Devaney was now up in the athletic director's booth and Johnny Rodgers was playing in Canada and Tom Osborne was on the sidelines and Steve Runty, a well-liked career backup quarterback, would be starting against the mighty 10th-ranked Bruins.

They would feel much better a few hours later.

Could Osborne get it done? Would there be life after Devaney? Both questions were answered, however momentarily, with a resounding exclamation point in Nebraska's 40-13 victory over UCLA.

Johnny who? Okay, that's a stretch. But Randy Borg, the senior cornerback from Alliance, Neb., did a nice imitation of Rodgers with a 77-yard punt return for a touchdown that gave NU a 14-0 lead in the first quarter. And after a season without a reliable I-back, Tony Davis, a rugged sophomore from Tecumseh, Neb., offered hope

with 147 yards on 24 carries. Davis' tough running keyed two 80-yard scoring drives in the third quarter that all but killed the Bruins' chances. That would be a preview of Osborne teams to come.

Easily, the splash of the day came from Runty, the senior who played in place of starting senior Dave Humm, who was resting a knee injury. Runty, considered more of a runner, hit nine of 11 passes for 105 yards. He was efficient enough on this day.

Osborne's day. The tall red-head from Hastings, Neb., had passed his first test and showed he could work a bulletin board, too. Earlier in the week, UCLA quarterback Mark Harmon – of future TV and movie fame – was quoted as saying "Last year we had to play THEM. This year they have to play US." The quote found its way into the NU locker room; afterwards, defensive captain John Dutton said it fired up a young Blackshirt defense.

"This was probably the best prepared team, psychologically, of any team I've been around," Osborne said afterward.

Only one man was fresher mentally that day. He strode into the winning locker room after the game to shake hands and congratulate the players. His former players.

"That felt great," Devaney said. "It's a lot easier sitting up there (in the press box). It's a lot of fun."

At least now everyone knew the fun wasn't over.

Peterson (UCLA)

Norfleet (UCLA)

Runty (N)

Touchdown

Settles (UCLA)

Roberts (UCLA) D. Anderson (N)

Quarterback Steve Runty dives through a huge hole against the Bruins.

PASS

Meyer (M)

Tony Davis (N)

Ferragamo (N)

Jenkins (N)

Tony Davis catches a nine-yard pass from Vince Ferragamo in the first quarter against Missouri.

Red Zone

Red Zone Game 14

Nebraska 30, Missouri 7
Nov. 1, 1975

COLUMBIA, Mo. – Missouri got beat by Nebraska's Bummeroosky.

Bummerwho? Bummeroosky. It sounds like the name of a Cornhusker offensive lineman. Actually, it was the name of a play – a trick play that NU coach Tom Osborne referred to as "garbage" – that Nebraska used to escape Faurot Field with a 30-7 victory.

It wasn't Oklahoma. But in Osborne's early days, Missouri was an equal nemesis. Missouri gave Osborne his first loss, in 1973, and followed up by upsetting the Huskers again in 1974 in Lincoln. So here was Osborne, involved in another close Mizzou brawl, late in the second quarter with a vociferous crowd of 68,195 and national ABC audience watching closely. What could he do? It was time to take out the garbage.

Technically, it's a fake punt. Nebraska's players dubbed it the "Bummeroosky." Missouri coach Al Onofrio called it a "jackrabbit." It came with 1:46 left in the second quarter. With fullback Tony Davis handing the ball between John O'Leary's legs and the Nebraska offense going to the right and O'Leary unassumingly running to the left – 40 yards for a touchdown.

Onofrio had tried to alert his team of the fake punt. But the Tigers bit on the fake handoff to Monte Anthony.

The unorthodox play gave the Cornhuskers the breath-ing room for their defense to take control and other heroes to step up. Quarterback Vince Ferragamo found split Bobby Thomas for two touchdown passes in the second half. Defensive back Dave Butterfield intercepted a Steve Pisarkiewicz pass for Henry Marshall at the goalline.

"I don't think anybody can say we won on breaks," Osborne said. "We came up with some big plays and every time we threw some garbage at them, it worked."

Not that Osborne was apologizing for what his third-ranked team had to resort to to break the game open. All that mattered was Nebraska was 8-0 and headed for tune-ups with Kansas State and Iowa State before the annual Big Eight showdown with Oklahoma. Besides, who knows what a third straight loss to Mizzou would have done to Nebraska mentally?

"This was an awful big one for us," Osborne said. "We gained a lot of momentum and we still think we've got a good shot at it (Big Eight title). That's not to take anything away from Oklahoma, but they've still got three tough games, including Missouri here."

Marshall (M)

89

Butterfield (N)

INTERCEPTED
PASS

Stewart (M)

32

Monds (N)

26

Nebraska's Dave Butterfield steps in front of Mizzou's Henry Marshall to thwart a Tiger scoring attempt.

Red Zone

Red Zone Game 15

Nebraska 31, Alabama 24
Sept. 17, 1977

LINCOLN – The Big Red wasn't dead.

Was that even a question? Well, yes. Nebraska's place among the national powers was of major concern among Husker football fans. The Big Red hadn't beaten Oklahoma or won a Big Eight title since 1971. The Huskers went 9-3-1 in 1976, including a 4-3 record in the league. Now, to top it off, they had lost to Washington State and former Husker player and assistant Warren Powers in the 1977 season opener, 19-10, at home.

It was time for head coach Tom Osborne to make a statement. Or a stand. Or both.

But guess who's coming to dinner in week two? Alabama. And the Bear.

Nebraska 31, Alabama 24. Statement received.

It was a classic game, between an Alabama Tide with the young nucleus of talent (including running back Tony Nathan and receiver Ozzie Newsome) that would in two years win Bear Bryant's last national championship and a Nebraska team fighting for its name, pride and tradition. Could the Huskers still win the Big One?

They didn't get any bigger than this clash, played before 75,899 at Memorial Stadium and a national ABC-TV audience. Nebraska hadn't started a season 0-2 since 1957. The Tide was ranked third and fourth in the polls. But the Huskers, still smarting from the Wazzu loss, were pumped after watching "Star Wars" the Friday night before the game. The Bear trap was set.

And the force was with the Huskers. It was a brutally-physical game, with Alabama rushing for 232 yards and NU netting 238. Each team came from behind twice in the first half, which ended at 17-17, and the teams entered the fourth quarter tied at 24. Nebraska lost its quarterback, Tom Sorley, to a shoulder injury early in the game and had to win behind backup Randy Garcia.

But while true grit was all around, the game came down to a battle of true wit. The Bear vs. Osborne.

On this memorable day, Osborne earned his spurs, as the Bear would say. The Bear started first. On its second drive, the Tide had a first down at the NU 40 when quarterback Jeff Rutledge handed off to Nathan, who flipped the ball back to Rutledge, who then found Newsome for a 33-yard gain to set up a touchdown.

Osborne's turn. Trailing 7-3, Osborne called a halfback pass from I-back Rick Berns and another flea flicker that had NU knocking on the Tide's goal line. Finally, on fourth down, Osborne tried a daring move: a fake field goal in which Randy Garcia, the holder, took the snap, avoided the rush and found Berns for a touchdown.

It seemed like Husker I-back Rick Berns always had a jersey torn as he was lunging ahead for more yards. Here, Berns lunges for a touchdown against Alabama.

Red Zone

Back and forth they went, with Berns leading the way. The tough, slashing junior rushed for 129 yards and three touchdowns, including the clincher from one-yard that capped a breathtaking 80-yard drive with 7:12 left that gave NU its 31-24 lead.

But Osborne showed he was a quick learner. In the final seven minutes, Alabama twice went for the double-hand-off with Rutledge throwing deep passes. Both times, NU monster back Jim Pillen was there to intercept.

Later, in an emotional locker room, the team presented Osborne with the game ball.

"This came at an awful good time," Osborne said. "Our players played with confidence and poise. If you play well and lose, pretty soon you'll keep losing."

The day was complete when Osborne got a tip of the Bear's houndstooth hat.

"I think we lost to a good team," Bryant said. "I'd like to think that time ran out on us but I guess that's being optimistic. Nebraska did a real fine job and really rose up when they had to. Nebraska richly deserved to win the game, to tell you the truth.

"I don't know how good they are because I don't know how good – or bad – we are. We all learned a lot today but don't ask me what. When you play Nebraska you are bound to learn some and I hope we did."

What everyone learned was that Big Red wasn't dead.

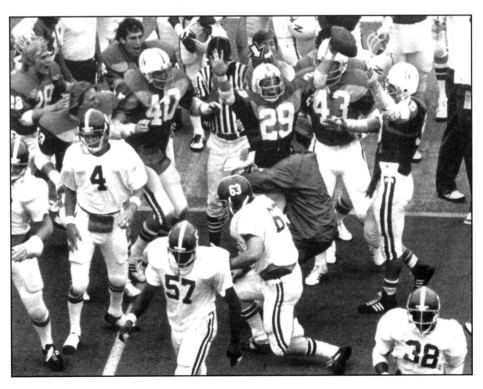

Nebraska safety Jim Pillen had his share of heroics in big games. Here, Pillen celebrates after intercepting a Jeff Rutledge pass to help beat Alabama.

Game 15

Red Zone Game 16

Nebraska 33, Colorado 15
Oct. 22, 1977

LINCOLN – The locker room was Times Square on New Year's Eve. Nebraska head coach Tom Osborne was hoisted on the shoulders of his players. Defensive coordinator Lance Van Zandt got a ride, too. Then, the entire Husker team started chanting, "Wal-ly! Wal-ly! Wal-ly!"

What's this? Another national championship? Osborne's first Big Eight title? His first win over Oklahoma?

Nah. Just another victory over Colorado.

Huh? Please, allow an explanation. Nebraska's 33-15 win was not your typical Nebraska victory over the Big Eight team-of-the-weak. This was Colorado, which had represented the Big Eight in the Orange Bowl the previous year. This was Colorado, with the Big Eight's leading offense, directed by quarterback Jeff Knapple. Mostly, this was Colorado, which had big, bad Ruben Vaughan, who didn't want to wait for Bill McCartney to get the CU job in 1982. Vaughan, considered the best defensive tackle in the league, wanted to hate the Huskers now. That's exactly what he said in not-so-many-words to the media that week.

The comments by Vaughan, who was way ahead of his time, served as a rallying point for the Huskers, who apparently weren't slapped to attention the previous week by Iowa State, which had marched into Lincoln and stolen a 24-21 upset victory over the Big Red. Vaughan's comments were taped on the floor of the Husker locker room so that each player could stomp on them as he left for the field. Whatever works.

The problem was, not all 100-plus Huskers would get a shot at Vaughan. The big Buff was one man's task alone: offensive guard Stan "Wally" Waldemore. Old Wally never did score a touchdown or make an interception that day. But this was his day. Waldemore was credited widely with neutralizing Vaughan, who had nine tackles and was not a factor. The 6-4, 260-pound senior from Belleville, N.J., blushed from the attention given by his teammates when they noticed a TV camera pointed at him in the locker room.

"This has to be the greatest thrill in my life," Waldemore said. "I will remember that all of my life. It was pretty emotional for a minute."

It got downright hairy in the second quarter, when Knapple threatened to break the game open. But tiny Nebraska safety Larry Valasek stepped in front of CU tight end Bob Niziolek at the NU 16 and pulled off the interception. Colorado would never threaten again. And NU, behind – who else? – Waldemore, cranked out season highs of 390 yards rushing and 480 in total offense. Sophomore I-back I.M. Hipp scored twice, including a 28-yard run off a perfect audible call by quarterback Tom Sorley for a 16-15 halftime lead.

The victory kept the Huskers' slim Big Eight title hopes alive and, more importantly, kept them from falling back into the pack a second straight year. And, for another decade, it would quiet the herd out west.

"Everybody was fired up," Waldemore said. "The Colorado fans were yelling "Ruben, Ruben, Ruben' before the game. But I think we all handled them pretty well. That quote of his doesn't mean anything now."

Game 16

Finally, it was time to
celebrate after an
Oklahoma game.

Red Zone

Red Zone Game 17

Nebraska 17, Oklahoma 14
Nov. 11, 1978

LINCOLN – Finally.

The raucuous celebration that followed Nebraska' 17-14 victory over Oklahoma – with the Memorial Stadium goalposts being torn down for the first time since 1959 – was born from as much relief as elation. Ding, dong, the Oklahoma Sooners were dead. Finally.

And nobody was more relieved than the Biggest Red himself, Nebraska coach Tom Osborne, who hadn't beaten Oklahoma since he took over the program in 1973. The whispers from Omaha to Ogallala were loud and clear: maybe Osborne couldn't cut it if he couldn't beat OU. The whispers were loud enough to chase Osborne to Boulder, Colo., for a post-season job interview. But on this day, Osborne was a hero. Finally. This was his game-of-the-century.

"I would say this was the biggest game we've ever had because of what it means," said Osborne, who could have been, and probably was, talking about himself.

The national ABC game had all the thrills and, for the Sooners, spills of a classic. Folks in every corner bar in every corner of Nebraska still talk about this game with a reverence. They remember every big play in this game. And, if they allow their memories to harken closer, they can still hear every big hit.

It was that kind of game. Big hits. Big plays. That was

how Nebraska would have to beat the fleet Sooner machine. Osborne and his staff knew it. Oklahoma was ranked No. 1 and many felt this was the Sooners' best team in decades. OU, with polished option quarterback Thomas Lott and 1978 Heisman Trophy winner Billy Sims and David Overstreet and Kenny King, had more speed than an Olympic track team. Ditto for the Sooners' defense. So the Huskers went with the KISS plan: Keep it simple, stupid.

Offensively, the Huskers planned to take it right at Oklahoma, which played a soft middle. NU wore out the famed "Iso" play – with fullback Andra Franklin leading the way for I-backs Rick Berns (113 yards) and I.M. Hipp. Franklin, a sophomore, had the game of his life, blocking All-America linebackers Daryl Hunt and George Cumby and even making 12 huge yards on a draw that set up the winning field goal by Billy Todd in the fourth quarter.

On the other side, the Blackshirts had one plan: Knock the Sooners back to Bartlesville, without a ticket. NU coaches knew they couldn't keep OU's speed down all game. So they tried to force mistakes. Speed vs. Muscle. It worked to bone-crunching perfection. Oklahoma fumbled the ball nine times and lost six. But it was two that didn't count and the last one that did that was all anyone in Nebraska red wanted to talk about. And still do.

The Huskers were up, 14-7, in the third quarter when Lott fumbled on fourth-and-one and monster Jim Pillen – who was a scary sight for Sooner fans this day – recovered. Oops. The officials said the Huskers were offsides. Next play: Sims rushed 30 yards for a game-tying touchdown.

Then, after Todd's field goal with 11:51 left, Nebraska thought it got the break of the game when OU's Kelly Phelps returned the kickoff and Husker linebacker John Ruud laid out Phelps – and the ball – with a hit so violent it should have had an "R" rating. Oops again. The officials ruled that Phelps had been down, when replays – and every Elks Club in Nebraska can confirm this – showed the knee was not down yet. Oh, the Huskers could have had the ball on the OU 17. Were Nebraskans going to be cursing the officials all winter?

Not to worry. Oh, sure, the Sooners were driving again late in the game and Sims was gliding through red creases and Barry Switzer was rubbing his rabbit's foot. But this time might was right. After a 17-yard gain to the Nebraska 3-yardline, which in itself broke nearly every heart in the place, it was Pillen and safety Jeff Hansen to the rescue. Hansen delivered the game-deciding, ball-jarring hit on Sims. Pillen smothered the ball. There was 3:27 remaining. The Huskers, for one week anyway, were now ranked No. 2 and looking ahead to a national title bout with top-ranked Penn State.

The photo in the next day's *World-Herald* belongs in some kind of Big Red museum. It shows Pillen, No. 29, discovering Sims' offering and about to pounce on it as if it were the winning $84 million lottery ticket lying on the ground. In a way, it was. Osborne, and Nebraska, finally hit the Big Eight lotto. But this was worth so much more than money.

"I've been doing a lot of talking," Pillen said in the victorious locker room when a new wave of reporters came at him. "But I don't mind. I could probably talk all night about this game. I probably will, too."

Red Zone

Rick Berns goes for four of his 113 yards against OU.

Larry Cole sacks Missouri quarterback Phil Bradley.

Red Zone

Red Zone Game 18

Nebraska 23, Missouri 20
Nov. 3, 1979

COLUMBIA, Mo. – The Huskers were ranked No. 2 in the nation. They were cruising, at 7-0, toward another end-of-the-world showdown at Oklahoma. But first, there was some unfinished business.

There was Missouri.

The Tigers had always been a thorn in Nebraska's overalls, but now, with Mizzou head coach Warren Powers around to stir the pot, the blood pressure in Nebraska was up a few notches. Powers, a former NU defensive back under Bob Devaney and assistant coach under Devaney and Tom Osborne, modeled his program after NU. He rebuilt the weight room, hired former Huskers for his staff and even had his scout team wear red during "Nebraska week."

Powers had a psychological thing going, too: he had beaten the Huskers two straight years – with Washington State in 1977 and Missouri in 1978. The latter was unforgiveable. It came a week after NU's emotional victory over Oklahoma and knocked the Huskers out of the 1978 national title race and, worse, into an Orange Bowl rematch with OU.

But settling scores with Mizzou was never an easy thing. Not this time, either.

Never mind that MU entered the game with an underachieving 4-3 record. The Tigers were ready to make

their season on this sun-splashed day. What transpired was a typical Nebraska-Missouri back-alley brawl. NU, on touchdown runs from I-back Jarvis Redwine and quarterback Tim Hager and field goals of 24 and 26 yards from Dean Sukup, led 17-6 at the half. Easy going?

Nothing doing. The Tigers brought the second-largest crowd in Faurot Field history (74,575) to its feet with a 14-point explosion. After a touchdown pass from Phil Bradley to Andy Gibler, MU's two-point conversion play failed. But on the kickoff Ron Fellows jarred NU returner Anthony Steels and the ball popped out and into the welcome arms of Mizzou's Orlando Pope, who returned it 17 yards for a touchdown. This time, Bradley got it right, completing the two-point conversion to tie the score after three quarters.

Time to panic? No. Time for Jeff Quinn. NU coach Tom Osborne brought the backup quarterback off the bench because he knew the big, strong Quinn could get some yards on the option – especially with the Tigers overplaying the pitch. Quinn did just that and woke the Husker offense out of its nap on a drive that included 10 straight running plays before Sukup nailed the game-winning 19-yarder.

But the Huskers scored too quickly. Bradley still had a few minutes. The elusive Tiger junior hit eight passes on a desperate drive that stalled at the Huskers' 11 with three seconds left. Time out, Mizzou. What to do? Kick the field goal and walk off with a moral victory over the No. 2-ranked team? Or go for the win over the coach and team that Powers loved to beat. Powers couldn't help himself. He went for the win.

But this year, James Wilder, the bullish Missouri fullback who had busted down Nebraska dreams a year ago, could not be found. Wilder was knocked to the ground on a pass route. Bradley never saw him. The only thing he saw was defensive end Derrie Nelson's wild eyes as he was buried under in a 18-yard sack.

"Anybody back in Nebraska not happy with this win doesn't know what happened down here," Osborne said.

Later, Osborne would be trying to find out more about what happened. Redwine, the Big Eight's leading rusher, had been knocked out of the game in the second quarter with a sore knee. Redwine later complained that a Tiger defender, Norman Goodman, had purposely tried to take out his knee while Redwine was blocking on an extra point. For most of that week, Powers and Osborne traded jabs in the newspapers.

Nebraska had won this battle. But the war with Missouri was just beginning.

Red Zone

Fellows (M)   Sukup (N)

Goodman (M)

Dean Sukup boots a 19-yard field goal with 3:15 left to give the Huskers' the winning margin over Missouri.

The Huskers had a
fine Redwine, as in
Jarvis, to beat Penn
State in Happy Valley.
Here, Redwine flies
over from three yards
for a 13-0 lead.

Red Zone

Red Zone Game 19

Nebraska 21, Penn State 7
Sept. 27, 1980

UNIVERSITY PARK, Pa. – To this day, Derrie Nelson says the 1980 Blackshirts were the best defense in Nebraska history.

It's hard to argue with Nelson, a defensive end on that unit, and not just because he still looks big enough to bury you noggin-first into the turf. The 1980 Husker defense, led by Nelson and Jimmy Williams and Henry Waechter and Curt Hineline and Sammy Sims and Russell Gary, allowed only 8.45 points per game that season. That ranked No. 2 in the nation. And that ranked among the alltime lowest in NU history, along with the 1964 (7.5 points allowed per game), 1966 (8.4), 1967 (8.3), 1971 (8.2) and 1972 (8.3) units.

What's more, the 1980 Blackshirts did it against a schedule that included Iowa, Penn State, Florida State, Missouri and Oklahoma. And they did it without a typically-potent Nebraska offense.

No game illustrated the power of the 1980 Blackshirts better than the Huskers' 21-7 victory at Penn State.

Considering the setting – third-ranked Nebraska playing before a national TV audience and 84,585 at Beaver Stadium (the largest crowd for a Nebraska game since the 1941 Rose Bowl) – and the fact that 11th-ranked Penn State had future NFL-types like quarterbacks Jeff Hostetler and Todd Blackledge and running back Curt Warner on the field and NU coughed up three turnovers and had 141 yards in penalties, this was one of the greatest – if not the best – defensive game in Nebraska history.

Inside the Nittany Lion locker room, there were two signs that read, "Outlasta Nebraska" and "There will be no Redwine before its time." But it was the Nebraska defense that was vintage stuff on the Huskers' first trip into Happy Valley.

Consider the numbers. Outlandish numbers. The Blackshirts pillaged Joe Paterno's offense for seven turnovers – four times on fumbles and three interceptions. After Penn State scored on a 74-yard drive in the second quarter to cut the Husker lead to 14-7, four of the eight Penn State drives in the second half ended in turnovers. Hostetler, then a sophomore and Blackledge, a redshirt freshman, were sacked a combined nine times for losses of 89 yards. That's right. Nine sacks.

This was one for the Big Red library, complete with bookends. Defensive ends Nelson and Williams. Nelson had two sacks, five tackles and recovered a fumble that led to Nebraska's first touchdown. Williams, a walk-on from Washington D.C. playing in front of his father, also had two sacks and five tackles. All told, the Nittany Lions were held to 13 first downs, 123 yards passing and, thanks to the yardage losses, a meager 33 yards rushing.

Even when the Lions got something going late, with Blackledge and Warner leading Penn State to the Nebraska 11, an end-around to Kenny Jackson was stopped for a 14-yard loss. Of course, Jackson fumbled. Middle guard Jeff Merrell recovered for the Blackshirts, who could do little wrong.

Meanwhile, the Nebraska offense was just good enough. Jarvis Redwine, the senior I-back and Heisman hopeful, padded his resume with 189 yards before the East Coast media and national tube.

"The only other player we've had with as much talent was Johnny Rodgers and he DID win the Heisman Trophy," NU head coach Tom Osborne told the Eastern media afterwards. "Jarvis certainly deserves the recognition."

Only because a defense can't win the Heisman.

Red Zone

Waechter (N)

Blackledge (PS)
FUMBLED

Before he would go on to star as Penn State's quarterback, Todd Blackledge took his lumps. Here, Nebraska's Henry Waechter provides some of the lumps.

The early scoring explosion: quarterback Turner Gill with I-back sidekick Mike Rozier against Auburn in 1981.

Red Zone

Red Zone Game 20

Nebraska 17, Auburn 3
Oct. 3, 1981

LINCOLN – A crowd of 76,423 – the largest ever for a Nebraska non-conference home game – sat through a dreary, rainy Saturday afternoon in Memorial Stadium on Oct. 3, 1981. The fans must have known that something was up.

They must have sensed that Nebraska vs. Auburn was more than just your basic clash of college football cultures. Somehow, the faces beneath the soaked red ponchos must have known this was an important crossroads day for the Husker program.

This was a program that had won a handful of big games – UCLA in 1973, Alabama in 1977, Oklahoma in 1978, Penn State in 1979-80 – but hadn't won an outright Big Eight title since 1972. This was a program whose coach, Tom Osborne, was trying to evolve his offense but was stalled in finding the right playmaker at quarterback. A program that had started the 1981 season by losing to Iowa, beating Florida State and losing to Penn State. A program that could ill afford to limp into the Big Eight at 1-3 and maintain any confidence or hope toward the immediate future.

Nebraska was a program that needed to see the future now. And on that soggy Saturday, that's what Husker fans saw.

His name was Turner Gill.

He had an average day, really. The sophomore quarterback came off the bench twice, in the second and fourth quarter, threw an interception and scored the Huskers' final touchdown. But the future was here and everyone in the place could sense it. Feel it. Gill was young, inexperienced, a raw, talented kid with a keen mind for running the option offense. He was Osborne's ticket to the future: a slick, quick and daring option-maker from Fort Worth, Texas, the kind Barry Switzer used to sign with a snap of his fingers. But not this time. Osborne stole one from Sooner Magic. Osborne knew Gill was special. All he needed was time. Well, the Huskers were running out of time. Gill's time was now.

But the future needed to wait on the present. Nebraska couldn't afford to lose to Auburn. Thankfully, the Blackshirts wouldn't allow it.

The Husker offense was as sloppy as the weather. Nebraska moved inside the Auburn 10 three times and didn't score. That's hard to do. No wonder when the Huskers left the field at halftime, trailing, 3-0, some of the fans in Memorial Stadium booed.

Crossroads, indeed.

Senior quarterback Mark Mauer, who had failed to convert a quarterback sneak on fourth-and-inches in the first quarter, started the second half. But it was more

Game 20

important that defensive end Jimmy Williams was on the field. Williams hit Tiger quarterback Charles Thomas and forced a fumble that Williams recovered on the Auburn four-yard line. Two plays later, Roger Craig scored to put NU on top, 10-3.

The Blackshirts – who held hard-running Auburn to 55 yards rushing – weren't done. Husker safety Jeff Krejci recovered a Lionel James fumble at the Auburn nine-yard line midway through the fourth quarter. Gill, who had relieved Mauer by then, dropped back to pass and then tucked it away for an eight-yard touchdown run with 3:51 left.

That was the kind of play-making Osborne had in mind when he wooed Gill up north. The next two seasons, Gill, I-back Mike Rozier and wingback Irving Fryar would key one of the great offenses in college football history. Gill's presence brought a little sunshine to the rainy day people. But nobody was kidding themselves: Gill hadn't done much on this day except offer hope and a new beginning. The Blackshirts took a sock and stuffed it in the boo birds' mouths. Without the Blackshirts, the Huskers would have been all wet.

On Transition Saturday, Osborne chastised the fans for booing Mauer, saying "he's not our problem." Still, the Gill era had begun.

"I'm thankful for the way the players pulled together today," Osborne said. "We haven't had a whole lot of friends here last week and maybe not this week."

The sun would come out again. Camp Husker had a brand new best friend. His name was Turner Gill.

The teacher and the pupil: Tom Osborne discusses strategy with Turner Gill.

Game 20 79

After 59 minutes and 37 seconds of heroic, gutsy and nerve-racking football, Nebraska fullback Phil Bates follows Dean Steinkuhler (71) and looks to score and break the stalemate ...

Red Zone

Red Zone Game 21

Nebraska 6, Missouri 0
Oct. 24, 1981

COLUMBIA, Mo. – In the end, Nebraska's 6-0 victory over Missouri was as easy for Turner Gill as handing off to fullback Phil Bates.

But this day – Gill's "Hell Day" – was anything but easy.

This date will go down in history as one of the Huskers' great escapes and another chapter in the epic Nebraska-Missouri series, 59 minutes and 37 seconds of pushing and pulling and punting and defenses running off the field, victorious for the moment, arms held high and chests puffing, like heavyweight boxers taking a blow between rounds.

This was a game that had 72,001 locked tight in their bleacher seats and a captive regional TV audience that dared not leave the living room.

But this great Husker victory will also be known for its rite of initiation. For one unforgettable afternoon, Faurot Field was a Top Gun training site for Nebraska's top gun.

This was Hell Day for Gill, the sophomore quarterback who had been given the keys to the offense for the rest of the season (and his career). Missouri head coach Warren Powers, who always had something special planned for the Huskers, and defensive coordinator Carl Reese had come up with a brilliant scheme. They would blitz Gill, particulary on long-yardage situations, and see how much the young gun could take. Gill later estimated that the

Tigers blitzed him "20 to 25 times" but no one could blame Gill for not knowing the exact number. His head was spinning and he was the only Husker with green pants. And it was only halftime.

"He had more grass stains than I did," Nebraska junior center Dave Rimington said. "That's not a good sign."

There were plenty of other bad signs for both teams. It might have been a completely different game had Missouri's George Shorthose – who had gotten deep and was sprinting alone in the secondary – not dropped a sure touchdown pass on the Tigers' first possession. Both teams missed field goals, including Nebraska's Kevin Seibel, who was off from 26, 42 and 40 yards.

Meanwhile, the game almost came down to a chess match between Gill and Missouri safety Kevin Potter, the assigned hit man for the Tiger blitzes. A classic example came in the second quarter after the Huskers recovered a Tiger fumble on the MU 39. On the first play, Gill was sacked by Potter for a loss of eight. So much for that opportunity.

Part of Nebraska's problem was that the Huskers couldn't burn the Missouri blitz with passing (Gill was 1-of-9 in the first half) or on up-the-gut trap plays because the Tigers' defensive linemen were playing too tight. But then, somehow, it happened.

Game 21

81

The Huskers started what would be their last drive on their own 36 with 2:36 remaining. Missouri, for some reason, called off the blitz. Maybe the Tigers were playing prevent and hoping for a scoreless tie. Who knows? Later, Gill would call the strategy "a mistake." And he made them pay.

Gill completed three huge passes on the drive – 13 yards to Irving Fryar, and 24 and 21 yards to split end Todd Brown, the latter down to the Missouri four-yard line. On third down, Missouri gave Nebraska another break. The Tigers called time out.

Then, Rimington made a classic call. The play was a "34 trap." Since the Huskers had had problems splitting the defenders all day, Rimington called a "check" or "line audible" after having told Bates in the huddle to stay to the right.

Finally, all Gill had to do was hand off. Touchdown, Huskers, with 23 seconds left. The 15th-ranked Huskers moved to 3-0 in a huge win (because MU would beat Oklahoma that fall). In his previous two starts, Gill had coasted to 59-0 and 49-3 wins over Colorado and Kansas State. But now the Husker Top Gun had earned his stripes – his teammates' respect.

"Missouri really came after him, trying to shake him up," Bates said. "But he didn't budge one bit and he didn't crack. He has to be better than any quarterback in the Big Eight."

Gill was on his way, now that Hell Day was over.

Red Zone

... and for Nebraska center Dave Rimington (50), the sight of Bates scoring with 23 seconds left is one for sore eyes and muscles.

The Sooners and linebacker Jackie Shipp (49) are no match for the Huskers and Roger Craig on this early 19-yard scoring run – nor would they be all afternoon.

Red Zone

Red Zone Game 22

Nebraska 37, Oklahoma 14
Nov. 21, 1981

NORMAN, Okla. – All Mark Mauer wanted was a chance. One more chance.

Mauer had entered his senior year at Nebraska as the starting quarterback. Sure, he was no Jerry Tagge or Vince Ferragamo. But Mauer's worst trait was having the unfortunate timing of taking over the greatest offense in college football history – two years early. The Huskers' group of big-playmakers and All-America linemen were just pups in 1981. Under Mauer, the Huskers lost to Iowa in the opener. He was booed. NU started 2-2. Mauer was benched. He received hate mail. He felt banished. That's not how he wanted to finish his NU career, not how he wanted to relay the stories of his playing career to his kids years later. He prayed for one more opportunity to show what he could do.

On Nov. 20, in the wind-swept arena that is Owen Field, Mauer's prayers were answered.

Turner Gill, the brilliant sophomore who had taken over the job, had injured his leg the week before. He was out for the Oklahoma game, which wasn't the end-of-the-earth battle this year because the Sooners had fallen on hard times. Nebraska actually entered this game having already clinched the Big Eight championship. But now the national title was creeping into the picture. A win at Oklahoma and fifth-ranked Nebraska would play second-ranked Clemson in the Orange Bowl on New Year's

Night and you never know. But could they get there with Mauer?

Yes. Call it Mauer magic.

The senior played as if he were acting out his own script. He had the game of his career, completing 11-of-16 passes for 148 yards and a touchdown, helping the offense roll to 462 yards and leading Nebraska to a 37-14 victory. It was only the second win for Nebraska over OU in 10 years, the first in Norman since 1971 and the biggest blowout of the Sooners since 1969.

"Everybody is real happy," Nebraska coach Tom Osborne said. "Mark Mauer had a great day. For a guy who hadn't played much in a long time, we were very pleased with the poise and competitiveness he showed. Barry Switzer said afterward I ought to tell Mark he had a great ballgame."

Again, Mauer's support system was maturing and emerging as a national force. I-backs Mike Rozier (105) and Roger Craig (102) both went over 100 yards in the game. And the Blackshirts shut down a struggling Sooner offense. Oklahoma shocked the Huskers by scoring in six plays to open the game. But that was it. Nebraska retaliated by scoring the first three times it had the ball and, after Mauer's six-yard touchdown pass to Mitch Krenk, led 24-7 at halftime.

By then, some of the 74,087 had left the building and were headed down Lindsey Street toward "O'Connell's," where they would lament the Sooner downfall (5-4-1) with their favorite beverage.

Meanwhile, as the Huskers poured on 13 more points in the second half, the Mauer bandwagon was taking shape.

"Enough can't be said about Mark's performance," center Dave Rimington said. "When we really needed him he was there and that's the name of the game."

"A lot of people said that Mark wasn't that good. But I knew that Mark had it in him. He just needed another chance to show it."

Afterwards, as reporters crowded around his locker, Mauer said he knew Nebraska fans weren't quite as confident as Rozier. He knew the abuse would continue if he flopped. But he was willing to take the chance. He needed one more chance.

"I realized the people in Nebraska haven't been really happy with me," Mauer said.

"That's why I wanted to win this one so badly. It was definitely real nice for me, especially the way things have gone this year, to have the opportunity to do some things I wanted to do all year."

He snaps. He blocks. He tackles. Nebraska center Dave Rimington did it all, including bring down Buster Rhymes.

Red Zone Game 23

Nebraska 23, Missouri 19
Oct. 23, 1982

LINCOLN – They came with notepads and microphones and minicams draped over their shoulders. They came to Mike Rozier's locker because they had to see for themselves the warrior's face, wrinkled in pain and the badly-injured right hip. They came because they wanted to hear from the valiant I-back himself how one stays in a game and continues to run a football when he can't stand to run at all.

When the reporters got to Rozier's locker, he had just one request.

"Please, guys, don't make me laugh," Rozier said.

The line itself was funny. Except nobody around Nebraska was in the mood for laughter that afternoon.

It had little to do with Missouri's Tigers once again pushing the Huskers to the brink of defeat before NU survived another Tiger attack, 23-19. It had a lot to do with a native son named Randy Jostes and a certain "cheap shot" that knocked Husker quarterback Turner Gill out of the game.

This will always be known as the "Randy Jostes game" or the "cheap shot" game. All because late in the first half, with Missouri leading 7-6, Jostes, a defensive tackle for Missouri from Ralston, Neb., hit Gill from behind after the junior quarterback had already handed off and was jogging, according to *World-Herald* photos, with his hands down and clearly free of the ball.

Gill was taken to St. Elizabeth's Hospital with a concussion. Nebraska fans were incensed at the play. Unflappable Husker coach Tom Osborne was out on the field, hopping up and down and yelling at officials. The play would later cause a shouting match between Husker fans and Missouri coach Warren Powers after the game. For weeks, the debate raged on.

"He's fair game," Jostes said.

"I'm not going to ever have anything to say about it," Osborne said. "We've gone through this before. This is part of the game, I guess."

Yes, it was just one part of this game. A great game. As the *World-Herald's* Mike Kelly wrote the next day, "The hit on Gill spoiled a great college football game."

Indeed. This game is always known more for the Jostes hit than for being one of the gutsiest comebacks in Nebraska history, with most of the guts coming from Rozier and quarterback Bruce Mathison.

Mathison, a fifth-year senior from Superior, Wis., led Nebraska on two touchdown drives – both in the final five minutes of the game – including a 16-yard run to clinch the victory.

Game 23

87

But mostly, Mathison's job was simple: give the ball to Rozier. Gingerly.

Because of a hip pointer suffered the previous week, Rozier hadn't practiced all week and was listed as doubtful. But when Roger Craig went down early with an ankle injury, Rozier knew he had to play. He entered the game with 11:34 left in the second quarter. And he never left. Rozier wouldn't leave. They tried once to get him off but he waved off Jeff Smith.

The latter incident came late, with NU trailing 13-9 late in the fourth quarter and doomsday approaching the fifth-ranked Huskers. The Huskers drove 79 yards for a touchdown, with Rozier, somehow, running for 49 of them, including a 27-yard run down to the MU 1-yard-line. The play was called a "49-roll" and Rozier himself called it. The I-back was suggesting plays to Osborne – plays that would allow him to stay in the game. The roll plays, which go off-tackle, were ones he could handle.

It was after the 27-yard run that Rozier waved off Smith. Husker fans were glad. Fullback Mark Schellen would score the touchdown. And Rozier had provided a spark that quickly became a flame. Linebacker Brent Evans intercepted a Missouri pass. One play later, Mathison faked a pitch and ran 16 yards to make it 23-13.

The Tigers would score late, miss a two-point try and fail to recover an onside kick. Somehow, Nebraska had survived.

Somehow, Rozier had survived.

"Sure, it hurt," Rozier said. "But that's football. You're going to get hurt sooner or later. So you've got to learn to play with pain."

It was one of the most courageous performances in Nebraska history. Rozier would win the 1983 Heisman Trophy. But in so many ways, this might have been his greatest moment as a Cornhusker.

"I don't think anyone will ever realize the courage that Mike Rozier showed today," Osborne said.

Too bad it was overshadowed. In that regard, perhaps Jostes' play was even more of a cheap shot.

One play after he caught the "Bouncearooski" and passed to Mitch Krenk, Nebraska wingback Irving Fryar takes a pitch from Turner Gill and goes five yards to the Oklahoma 9-yard line.

With 8:27 left to play, Nebraska safety Dave Burke (33) jars the ball loose from Oklahoma's David Carter inside the Huskers' 5-yard line. Nebraska took over on downs one play later.

Red Zone

Red Zone Game 24

Nebraska 28, Oklahoma 24
Nov. 26, 1982

LINCOLN – First there was the Bummeroosky. Then the Fumblerooski.

Now Nebraska head coach Tom Osborne introduced the football world to the "Bounceroosky."

Hey, whatever works. And on a day of big plays from offenses that didn't rest until the turf looked like an Orange Julius, it was a little sleight of hand – or pass – from Osborne that helped make the difference.

And Nebraska's 28-24 victory over the Sooners did make a difference, despite the national picture. The Huskers were ranked third in the nation. They were shut out of the national championship, which would be decided between Penn State and Georgia in the Sugar Bowl on New Year's Day. All because of a late-drive comeback (and controversial catch) by Penn State that beat Nebraska earlier in the season.

But there still was much to accomplish for NU on this Friday-after-Thanksgiving Day game in bright red Memorial Stadium. Anytime Osborne and Barry Switzer got together it was news. But now Osborne could beat his nemesis for the first time in two straight seasons. He could make it a trend.

To do so, Osborne felt it necessary to dig into his bag of trick plays. Introducing the Bounceroosky, which was unveiled after Oklahoma had taken a 10-7 lead in the second quarter.

The play started with quarterback Turner Gill throwing a "lateral" pass to wingback Irving Fryar toward the sideline. The pass bounced to Fryar, positioned slightly behind Gill. The Sooner defense stopped. Incomplete pass, right? Wrong. The pass went backwards, making it a "lateral" and live ball. Fryar fielded the ball, turned and threw a 37-yard pass to tight end Mitch Krenk, who was downed at the OU 14. Nebraska scored two plays later.

Then things got really wild. After the Huskers rammed a 62-yard touchdown drive down the Sooners' throats for a 21-10 halftime lead, Oklahoma sent a warning to Nebraska: this game's only beginning. The not-so-subtle reminder came with Marcus Dupree chugging 86 yards for a touchdown to open the third quarter. More bad news: Nebraska I-back Mike Rozier had to leave the game with a reinjured ankle.

Not to worry. The Huskers had two I-backs in 1982, and Roger Craig came on to score the eventual game-winning touchdown, from three yards, for a 28-17 lead with 6:25 left. But Oklahoma fullback Stanley Wilson's one-yard touchdown cut the lead to 28-24 with 30 seconds left in the third quarter. Nebraskans still had 15 minutes – and the ghosts of nightmarish finishes against the Sooners – to deal with.

Then came the real trick of the day: the Blackshirts shut down an Oklahoma comeback in the fourth quarter. It helped that OU insisted on passing. Cornerback Dave Burke and safety Bret Clark both knocked down Kelly Phelps passes near the goal line on third and fourth down.

But the biggest hero was an unlikely one. Sophomore Scott Strasburger, a third-team defensive end playing as a linebacker in a special scheme designed for the game, stepped in front of a Phelps screen pass and intercepted. Strasburger ran to the Oklahoma 1-yard line with 26 seconds left, bringing the stadium to its feet and a barrage of oranges splattering to the turf. Oh, yes, and there were those few hundred or so fans who stormed the field and brought down the goalposts. With one second left. That's 15 yards on Nebraska. Good thing there was only one tick left. And good thing those fans didn't have to show up at Osborne's house that night for dinner.

"That (throwing oranges) is one of the most idiotic customs I've ever seen," an upset Osborne said afterwards.

The custom of going to the Orange Bowl was something Osborne would never tire of.

The sea of red converges on the turf – and Scott Strasburger (barely visible under a pile of fans) – after Strasburger's interception foiled the Sooners' last threat.

Red Zone

Despite complaining of slick footballs, Nebraska wingback Irving Fryar managed to hold onto this pass from Turner Gill for a 22-yard gain against LSU in the 1983 Orange Bowl.

Red Zone

Red Zone Game 25

Nebraska 21, LSU 20 (Orange Bowl)
Jan. 1, 1983

MIAMI, Fla. – Midway through his third Orange Bowl as Nebraska head coach, Tom Osborne was 0-2 on this storied stage and now his top-ranked offense had coughed up four first-half turnovers and was down to Louisiana State, 14-7. But at least someone had discovered the culprit.

"They were using Orange Bowl footballs out there," Nebraska wingback Irving Fryar said. "They were real slick and we couldn't hold onto them. It felt like they had plastic on them."

Call it the great Orange Bowl Football Theory. The Huskers would regroup and go on to win the 1983 Orange Bowl, 21-20. The turning point obviously came at halftime, when the Huskers talked the officials into using "Nebraska balls."

It was ugly, this first Osborne victory in the Orange Bowl. But how appropriate. Considering Osborne's tempestuous relationship with the Orange Bowl – he would play Oklahoma and Miami there and have his heart broken and rebroken into hundreds of tiny pieces by the football gods before winning his first national championship in the classic old structure – it was fitting that Osborne's first victory in the Orange Bowl would be like pulling teeth.

Even against an LSU team that was 8-3-1, had lost two of its last three regular-season games and was a 10 1/2-point underdog. But the Tigers of the Southeastern Conference were talented enough to take advantage of six turnovers. A Mike Rozier fumble with 6:43 left in the first quarter and a Fryar fumble in the second quarter (before the great switch) set up a pair of Dalton Hilliard one-yard touchdown runs that put the Tigers up by seven when the Huskers jogged into the locker room for some words of wisdom that were actually more of a reminder.

"Coach Osborne challenged us at halftime," Rozier said. "He said, "'You're supposed to be the best offense in the country; go out there and prove it.'"

That they did, before the smallest Orange Bowl crowd (54,407) since 1947, no doubt caused by the civil disturbances in the downtown projects area of Miami known as "Overtown" that provided a tense backdrop to Orange Bowl week. But those in attendance got a New Year's preview of big things to come on offense for Nebraska in 1983.

The Huskers, who outyarded LSU 403-211, were surprisingly balanced with 219 yards rushing and 184 passing – surprising for the nation's leading rushing team. But quarterback Turner Gill led a second-half comeback through the air. He hit Rozier with an 11-yard touchdown pass with 1:25 left in the third quarter that cut the LSU lead to 17-14.

Then, after LSU punter Clay Parker was forced to scramble by defensive end Tony Felici and was stopped short of the first down at the LSU 48, the Huskers needed just eight plays to take the lead for good. Gill then gave future opponents something to think about: on fourth-and-one, he play-action faked and threw an 18-yard pass to split end Todd Brown. Gill, who was 13-of-22 for 184 yards, later scored the go-ahead touchdown on a one-yard dive reminiscent of Jerry Tagge's touchdown to win the 1971 Orange Bowl and 1970 national title.

No such luck for the Huskers this night. And that's what kept the Orange Bowl victory celebration to a few handshakes. Penn State would win the national championship that day – the same Penn State that beat NU, 27-24, with a controversial play, back in September. A year earlier, Clemson had won the No. 1 ranking by beating Nebraska in the Orange Bowl. So the victory was dipped in frustration.

"We'd have liked to have played Penn State a little later down the road this season," Rozier said. "But there's nothing we can do about it now."

All they could do was wait until the next round with the Orange Bowl.

Turner Gill completes a pass in coach Tom Osborne's first Orange Bowl victory.

Red Zone

I-back Mike Rozier runs to the LSU 14, setting up a touchdown pass to him from Gill on the next play.

It didn't matter how many Nittany Lions were around, Penn State could not stop fullback Mark Schellen and the great Husker offense in the inaugural Kickoff Classic.

Red Zone Game 26

Nebraska 44, Penn State 6 (Kickoff Classic)
Aug. 29, 1983

East Rutherford, N.J. – Start spreadin' the news.

On a dark, rainy late summer's night in the Meadowlands, something rather large and scary rose out of the swamp. This Swamp Thing would go on to terrorize all of college football in 1983. It would earn the unofficial title of "the greatest team in college football history" by *Sports Illustrated*. It would set a plethora of NCAA offensive records. It would have a Heisman Trophy winner, and, actually, could have had two. And it would take a 12-0 record steaming down to the Orange Bowl for a date with destiny.

But first, the Nebraska football team had to win the Kickoff Classic.

The Huskers, the Big Red Swamp Thing, didn't just win the inaugural Kickoff Classic. They pillaged and plundered Penn State, 44-6. They dominated every aspect of the game, they even recovered eight of their own nine fumbles. Mostly, Nebraska sent a message on college football's version of Monday Night Football.

And that's what the Kickoff Classic was set up to do (Okay, there was the money thing): send a message. It was supposed to be a pre-season bowl game, preferably between two of the top teams in the pre-season polls and, if they got lucky, two teams who never got to meet in the previous year's bowls. The first Kickoff Classic struck it

rich in terms of marquee value: Penn State was defending national champion. Nebraska wanted revenge on the Lions after losing, 27-24 – and losing on a controversial catch. If not for that game, Nebraska might have won the national title. The Huskers couldn't get it back on this Monday night outside the Big Apple. They couldn't even play the same Penn State team; this version was much younger and inexperienced, especially at quarterback. What the Huskers had to do was play for the future.

The future looked as bright as the Broadway lights shining in the distance.

All of Nebraska seemed on stage. The Huskers were No. 1 in the pre-season polls for the first time since 1976. And Nebraska Gov. Bob Kerrey was causing a media stir by appearing with his new friend, actress Debra Winger. They had come to see a show. It would be a hit.

But not immediately. Here's how it started. Mike Rozier fumbled the opening kickoff. NU's first play from scrimmage was a busted play for a loss of eight yards. The Huskers failed to make a first down on their first drive. So much for omens.

The "Scoring Explosion" was just stuck in traffic in the Lincoln Tunnel. They would appear. The focus, of course, was on quarterback Turner Gill, I-back Mike Rozier and wingback Irving Fryar – named the "triplets" by Oklahoma coach Barry Switzer – and the trio didn't disappoint. They led the Huskers to a 21-0 halftime lead on three impressive drives and an offense that would total 500 yards, including 322 on the ground. Gill was the star. He completed 11-of-14 passes for 158 yards and a touchdown and ran 13 times for 53 yards and another touchdown and earned a kiss from Winger and a Heisman stump from Lee Corso, the future ESPN analyst who, in 1983, did the color for the TV broadcast of the Kickoff Classic.

"He's the most valuable player I've seen on a football team in a long time," Corso told the *World-Herald* after the game. "Right now, he's got to be the leading candidate for the Heisman Trophy."

Even then, Corso's predictions were just a tad, well, off-center. Rozier would win the Heisman. It just went to show that the Huskers had any number of weapons to deploy against opponents. And this night proved that the Huskers were more com-

plete than anyone had imagined before the game. The Blackshirts, thought to be a weak link, were a pleasant surprise, holding Penn State scoreless until the final 20 seconds and coming up with a big play – linebacker Mike Knox's 27-yard interception return for a touchdown. Monte Engebritson and Todd Frain, who each caught

As if the Nebraska offense wasn't enough, the Blackshirts pitched in with this 27-yard interception for a touchdown by linebacker Mike Knox against Penn State.

Red Zone

touchdown passes, eased the worries about the tight end position. And the four new players on the offensive line, including center Mark Traynowicz, earned everyone's praise after dominating the Lions.

"I was just amazed," head coach Tom Osborne said. "I had no idea at all we'd win like this."

Think how Penn State coach Joe Paterno felt. The 38-point loss equaled the worst loss of JoePa's brilliant career (17 years to that point).

"Nebraska was a great football team tonight," Paterno said. "They beat us in every way. We got outcoached.

"Did you ever get the crap kicked out of you? Well, you just saw Penn State get the crap kicked out of it."

Paterno, though, would not be alone in 1983. The Swamp Thing left New York with an unexpected aura. If the Huskers could make it there, they could make it anywhere.

Turner Gill may have been the star of the Kickoff Classic, but I-back Mike Rozier would dive into the 1983 Heisman Trophy race.

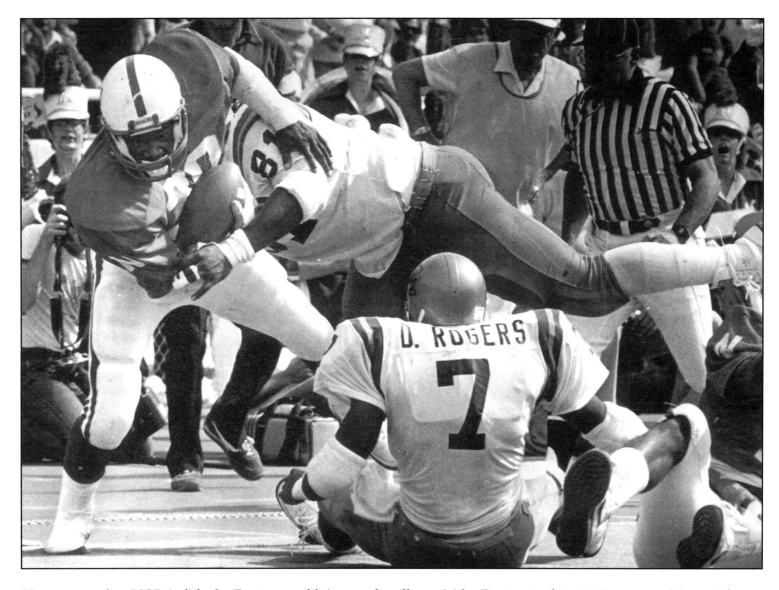

No matter what UCLA did, the Bruins couldn't get a handle on Mike Rozier in this 1983 game at Memorial Stadium.

Red Zone Game 27

Nebraska 42, UCLA 10
Sept. 24, 1983

LINCOLN – The numbers that made Nebraska's 42-10 victory over UCLA memorable were "2" and "100."

The fourth game of the 1983 season was Nebraska coach Tom Osborne's 100th career victory – in his 11th season. But it will be remembered more for Mike Rozier's two-yard touchdown run.

It was two yards, right?

Well, technically, yes. But Rozier probably should have had 60 more yards tacked onto his total after he ad-libbed more than Jay Leno on a second-quarter touchdown run.

It started with the Huskers clinging to a 14-10 lead. On third down at the UCLA 2-yard line, Rozier took a pitch from quarterback Turner Gill. Rozier started to his left. But waiting for him in the backfield was UCLA's Ron Pitts. Rozier didn't like that option, so he changed directions and backtracked to the 18. Yes, the 18.

He looped around several Bruin defenders and finally beat a path into the right corner of the end zone. It looked like something out of the Marx Brothers' college football movie "Horsefeathers."

"That's the finest two-yard run I've ever seen," Osborne said.

Indeed, it was one of the great runs in Rozier's career. Definitely, the best two-yard run of his life.

"He's inhuman," said Nebraska linebacker Mark Daum of Rozier. "I saw him turn back and said, "Oh, no!' He's going to take a 15-yard loss. He plain outran everybody."

Rozier's touchdown was more than just breathing room for the top-ranked Huskers. It was part of a 42-point scoring explosion in a span of 28 minutes that ended when cornerback Dave Burke returned an interception for a score with 8:59 left in the game.

So much for UCLA's 10-0 lead. But that was only a matter of time. The Huskers had their way with the Bruins' defense, rushing for 477 yards and passing for 123.

It actually could have been worse. Nebraska had one touchdown called back – a 24-yard run by Rozier (who had 159 yards and two touchdowns) – by a holding penalty. And on the last play of the game, Osborne instructed quarterback Craig Sundberg to down the ball on the UCLA 2-yard line as time expired. He could have just had Rozier take the ball and run around some more.

In a sense, Rozier's run was very symbolic on a milestone day for Osborne, who received a rousing ovation from the south stands at Memorial Stadium after the game and got the game ball in the locker room. It had been a long, winding career already for Osborne at Nebraska: 100 wins in 10-plus seasons but plenty of big losses to Oklahoma and unhappy fans, a short look at the Colorado job, a change in offensive philosophy (toward the option) and now a big leap in recruiting. The 1983 team was Osborne's best by many– Sports Illustrated had called it "The Greatest College Football Team in history" – because Osborne had upgraded his talent pool. He had talent that could score sideline-to-sideline on a two-yard run. Talent to score 42 points just like that. And that seemed to be the message Osborne sent as the world of Big Red stopped to applaud his job well done. So far.

"Everybody is looking at me and says "What is this guy, some kind of weirdo?" Osborne said afterwards. "I'm pleased to have won 100 games but I haven't won them. I have never won a game and that's my sincere feeling because I don't play. The players win the games."

Red Zone Game 28

Nebraska 69, Colorado 19
Oct. 22, 1983

LINCOLN – Long before there was HuskerVision or a "Husker Authentics" shop across from Memorial Stadium, this is how they marketed the Nebraska football team: the athletic department would put out a poster. Fans would stream into the sports information office to buy one. Players, coaches, everybody had to have a Husker football poster.

Well, the 1983 poster remains a classic. It was a shot of the scoreboard high above the Memorial Stadium north end zone. Bursting out of the scoreboard were Nebraska quarterback Turner Gill, I-back Mike Rozier and wingback Irving Fryar above the title, "The Scoring Explosion."

That was the 1983 team. It still holds NCAA records for touchdowns and points scored in a season. It could score from the locker room.

No game illustrated that awesome power more than the Colorado game on Oct. 22, 1983.

The Huskers were in trouble. Well, maybe not big trouble. They were only up, 14-12, over the Buffs. But these weren't the Bill McCartney Buffs who would terrorize Nebraska in the late 80s and early 90s. No. These were the Bad News Buffs who couldn't decide on an offense and almost got McCartney fired later that year. That was part of the problem on this day. McCartney caught NU

coaches by surprise when he came out with a one-back set with two tight ends and two flankers and not the I-formation NU had worked on. The Huskers couldn't stop CU. And the Husker offense had this bad habit, maybe out of boredom, of diddling around and throwing on the switch whenever it wanted.

Nobody who was in Memorial Stadium that day will forget when the switch went on.

Nebraska scored 48 points in the third quarter. That's right. Seven touchdowns, in one quarter. The Huskers scored so quick that reporters and officials didn't have time to see if this were some kind of record. Almost. Nebraska would have tied the NCAA record of 49 in one quarter (owned by Davidson and Houston) had kicker Scott Livingston not missed an extra point. Oh, well. His foot was probably tired.

The only thing that didn't happen in this amazing third quarter were Gill, Rozier and Fryar actually bursting through the scoreboard. As it was, the scoreboard was like a pinball machine ringing up the points. Ding! Ding! Ding!

It was this easy:

The "Triplets" started it off with a relay-team touchdown on the second play of the second half. Gill handed off to Rozier, who gave the ball to Fryar on a reverse – 54 yards for a touchdown.

Colorado then tried a fake punt at the Colorado 23 and was stopped short. Three plays later, Rozier scored from 13 yards.

CU fumbled the kickoff and Nebraska's Scott Strasburger recovered at the CU 28. Two plays later, Gill scored on a 17-yard run.

Nebraska's Rob Stuckey intercepted a Steve Vogel pass at the Colorado 34. First play, Gill hit Fryar for a 34-yard touchdown pass.

On its next possession, Colorado went for it on fourth down and threw an incomplete pass. Nebraska first down at the CU 43. Three plays later, Rozier scored from 18 yards.

CU fumbled the kickoff. Nebraska recovered at the CU 14. Two plays later, I-back Jeff Smith scored from 12 yards.

Colorado went three and out. Punted the ball 20 yards out of bounds to the CU 48. Five plays later – the longest drive of the quarter – backup quarterback Nate Mason hit Shane Swanson for a one-yard touchdown pass.

Nebraska 62, Colorado 12. There was still 2:47 left in the third quarter.

"I kept looking up at the scoreboard and it was still the third quarter," said NU defensive back Mike McCashland. "I couldn't believe it."

Believe it. All seven touchdowns required fewer than 18 plays and possession time of 4:14. That had to be a record of some kind. Actual records that were set that day were most points by a Nebraska team at home and the Big Eight mark for points scored in a half (55). Certainly, the Buffs deserved a big assist for the outburst. But the depth and power of how Nebraska took advantage was the story of the day, a day when a poster came to life.

Please take a photo, Colorado fans. This run by Guy Egging (stood up here by Nebraska's Dave Ridder) set up a Buff field goal for a 3-0 lead. Final score: Nebraska 69, Colorado 19.

Red Zone Game 29

Nebraska 28, Oklahoma 21
Nov. 26, 1983

NORMAN, Okla. – Of all the great names carved into this Mount Rushmore of a season – Gill, Rozier, Fryar, Steinkuhler – the keepers of Nebraska football history would have to find room for the name "Neil Harris," too.

Harris didn't fit the Husker "Rat Pack" of stars. For one, he played on defense, the much-maligned side of the ball in 1983, the unit that couldn't be trusted and was just along for the ride. He was a quiet junior cornerback from Kansas City, Kan. And two weeks prior to the 1983 Oklahoma game, Harris had lost his starting job. Who'd have thunk he would produce one of the biggest plays of this big season?

Nobody. But that's what happened as late-afternoon darkness had engulfed Owen Field on the Saturday after Thanksgiving. Harris and the Blackshirts combined to not only save the Huskers' bacon, but their eggs and hash browns, too. Talk about a full plate. All that was riding on this game was a third consecutive undefeated Big Eight season, an 11-0 record and a No. 1 ranking to take to the Orange Bowl.

That's all.

"The Big Eight, the national championship, it all flashed before my eyes before Neil's play," said Nebraska safety Bret Clark. "I was scared."

Sure, everyone in Nebraska red was scared. The Sooners were down and not going to a bowl. But Oklahoma coach Barry Switzer had made a stirring pre-game speech, gotten his troops fired-up and then saw them hold the "Scoring Explosion" to 28 points. And now, as darkness fell, OU quarterback Danny Bradley was making plays and the time on a dream season was ticking away madly.

Oklahoma started the final drive on its 26 with 5:12 left. If they scored, the Sooners could go for two and win or tie. Either way, NU's No. 1 ranking would be gone.

Bad sign: Harris, who started this game to help against the Sooners' running game, got beat during the drive on a 27-yard pass from Bradley to wingback Derrick Shepard. The crowd was on its feet. A sudden electricity filled the stadium. This was Oklahoma's bowl game. On the sidelines, and back home watching on TV, Nebraskans' heads were filled with all the worst fears and the old ghosts of the OU series. One very real ghost was on the field: Buster Rhymes, now a senior, who had scored late to beat NU as a freshman in 1980.

Oklahoma marched to the 3-yard line,but it was brought back by a motion penalty. Then Bradley was sacked by defensive end Bill Weber back to the 10, setting up third and fourth downs.

Where have you gone, Billy Sims? Bradley tried two passes. On third down he threw a slant-in pass to Shepard but it was broken up by Harris and monster back Mike McCashland.

Fourth down. And the Huskers had a clue where the play was going. Right cornerback Dave Burke told Harris in the huddle he thought the ball would go to Rhymes because he saw the receiver talking to Switzer on the sidelines.

"Their players do that," Burke said. "They get all antsy and they try to tell Switzer they can pull off a miracle."

No miracles this time, unless, of course, you count Harris tipping away the Bradley pass to Rhymes in the left corner of the end zone to preserve the victory, and more importantly, the shot at No. 1. But now nobody looked at the Blackshirts in those terms. They had earned some respect and trust. A lot.

"I'm glad the defense saved the day," said quarterback Turner Gill. "You've got to give the defense a lot of respect now. They won the game for us."

Early in another Nebraska-Oklahoma classic, the Huskers' Mike McCashland stops OU's Earl Johnson.

Red Zone Game 30

Nebraska 17, Oklahoma State 3
Oct. 6, 1984

LINCOLN – Here is every Nebraska boy's dream:

You get recruited by the Big Red Machine. Tom Osborne sits in your living room, eats a slice of your mother's blueberry pie and invites you to come to Lincoln. You make the team. You get to run out into Memorial Stadium, the third-largest city in your state on autumn Saturdays, with the chills running down your spine, through your arms and down into your toes. You work hard for four years and your parents and cousins and the hardware store manager from your small Nebraska town come out to every game, hoping to see you play. And, then, one day, it happens: you make a big play that wins the game for the Cornhuskers.

On Oct. 6, 1984, that boy was Shane Swanson.

Swanson was a senior wingback for Nebraska in 1984. Like many good Nebraska boys before him, Swanson had waited his turn – three years behind wingback legend Irving Fryar. Now here was Swanson, the prototypical Nebraska small-town kid, from Hershey, Neb. He was big into rodeo back in high school. That's why his nickname was "Cowboy."

With the ninth-ranked Oklahoma State Cowboys roping eighth-ranked Nebraska in a 3-3 tie going into the fourth quarter, it was Nebraska's Cowboy to the rescue.

Swanson didn't know it as he backed up to take Cary

Cooper's punt at midfield, midway through the fourth quarter, but his 15 minutes of fame were about to occur.

The sellout crowd at Memorial Stadium had been waiting for something big to happen all day. But the Cowboys, who would go into the last week of the season with a chance to win the Big Eight, were tough hombres to shake. Especially with Nebraska's offensive guns on the sidelines; I-backs Jeff Smith, Doug DuBose and fullback Tom Rathman all were out with injuries. And starting quarterback Craig Sundberg got benched after three interceptions.

This wasn't exactly what Husker fans needed to soothe their anxieties one week after the formerly No. 1-ranked Huskers had been upset at Syracuse. As the fourth quarter began, they began to wonder: Would Nebraska lose two straight for the first time since 1976?

And then Cooper punted.

Swanson took the punt at the OSU 49, shot up the middle, angled to his right and jetted to the end zone for a touchdown. With 8:51 left in the game, the Huskers had their first lead, 10-3. Just like that. The crowd went crazy. Swanson was the hero.

"It was awesome. That was the icebreaker," said quarterback Travis Turner, who relieved Sundberg in the second quarter. "We needed a big play. We hadn't had one all day. It really helped put us over the edge."

There were other big plays on a rare day of drama at Memorial Stadium. A 43-yard touchdown pass from Oklahoma State quarterback Rusty Hilger to split end Malcolm Lewis was called back because of a clipping penalty by guard Derek Burton against NU corner Dave Burke, who had no shot to catch Lewis when he was clipped. Burke was everywhere on this day. Besides seven tackles and an interception and fumble recovery, Burke threw a big block on Swanson's return and deflected a 42-yard field goal attempt by OSU when it was 10-3.

But the play that was frozen in every fan's mind as they left the stadium that day – the play that defined this great victory – was Swanson's punt return. Only in Nebraska, where small-town boys grow up with big dreams, do these kinds of fairy tales become real life.

"There isn't a better person, a person that's more deserving of that punt return than Shane Swanson," said Husker linebacker Mark Daum, another small-town Nebraskan. "He's a down-to-earth kid, a hardworking kid. He's tough."

Somewhere, the next Shane Swanson was watching, listening and dreaming.

A nice shot of the Nebraska offense, unfolding against Missouri, with I-back Doug DuBose taking the pitch from Travis Turner (14) and looking for a crease on a 22-yard touchdown run.

Red Zone

Red Zone Game 31

Nebraska 28, Missouri 20
Oct. 19, 1985

COLUMBIA, Mo. – How do you stop a kick?

That's what the Missouri Tigers were asking themselves after another wild and wacky afternoon in the Nebraska vs. Missouri series. It didn't seem to matter that Husker tormentor Warren Powers was gone from the Mizzou sideline and had been replaced by Woody Widenhofer. The Tigers, once again, were poised for an upset over Nebraska.

But this time, Missouri could have kicked itself – if Dale Klein hadn't already done the honors.

The Tigers stopped the sputtering Nebraska offense all day. Bad day at the office? Good thing the Huskers brought Klein, a junior walk-on from Seward, Neb., along for the ride. Klein saved the day with an NCAA record seven field goals in Nebraska's 28-20 win.

It was like a broken record for the Huskers, who rushed for 320 yards but couldn't break a fired-up Mizzou defense that would only bend. Nebraska would drive. Missouri would make a big play. Klein would make a bigger kick.

He made them from 32, 22, 43, 44, 29, 43 and 43 yards. And then he went looking for the nearest whirlpool.

"I didn't really care about the record," Klein said. "I just wanted us to win the game."

That it took Klein's magnificent seven to beat Missouri was incredible. Unthinkable. After an opening-season loss to Florida State, the Huskers entered the MU game at 4-1 and ranked seventh in the AP poll. Missouri 0-5 was on its way to a 1-10 season under Widenhofer. But, as usual, the Tigers got up for Nebraska.

In fact, Missouri took a stunning 7-3 lead with 6:37 left in the first quarter when MU's Victor Moore beat cornerback Brian Davis and caught a 33-yard touchdown pass.

But Klein was just getting warmed up. After his initial 32-yarder, with 7:27 left in the first quarter, he struck again after Moore's touchdown. Nebraska's Paul Miles ran 40 yards to the MU 11, the drive stalled and Klein hit a 22-yarder.

A 51-yard run by Doug DuBose and an interception by safety Chris Carr set up Klein's next two field goals, from 43 and 44 yards, for a 12-7 lead. Klein added an NCAA-record fifth in the first half with 1:29 left, from 29 yards, for a 15-7 lead.

The Huskers were playing with fire. Missouri, using short flare passes and scrambling rollouts by quarterback Warren Seitz, drove 73 yards in 10 plays to open the second half to cut the lead to 15-13. But a botched snap on the two-point converstion was an omen – a bad one at that – for the Tigers. They would botch four center snaps and lose four turnovers – two interceptions and two fumbles.

But Mizzou would get one more chance in the second half. After Klein's set-up man, DuBose (who had a career-high 199 yards), ran 30 yards, Klein hit a 43-yard field goal for an 18-13 lead with 25 seconds left in the third quarter. Marlon Adler, who had replaced the injured Seitz, came in and fumbled a snap at the Tigers' 40. Nebraska linebacker Mike Knox recovered and, three plays later, DuBose finally broke the plane with a 22-yard touchdown run and 25-13 lead.

Klein would add one more field goal for insurance and NU needed all it could get. The Huskers were plagued with inconsistent quarterback play – McCathorn Clayton was 1-for-8 passing for 19 yards and two interceptions and was replaced in the third quarter by Travis Turner, who was 2-of-7 for 44 yards. But the Tigers had no answer for Klein's steady leg.

"We worked hard on stopping their running game," said Missouri safety Erik McMillan. "We worked hard on stopping their passing game. How hard can you work on stopping a kicker? I never thought it would come down to a kicker breaking an NCAA record."

In one of the great games of his great career, Nebraska defensive tackle Jim Skow puts pressure on Missouri quarterback Warren Seitz. Skow had four sacks for losses of 33 yards and eight tackles against Mizzou.

A Blackshirt zeroes in on a Florida State runner.

Red Zone

Red Zone Game 32

Nebraska 34, Florida State 17
Sept. 6, 1986

LINCOLN – The night before Nebraska's 1986 season-opener against Florida State, I went to a party at a writer's house in Lincoln. I remember it distinctly, not because of the cocktail weenies, but because several Husker fans there were wearing black armbands with "NCAA" and the circle-slash sign through it. Others wore buttons that read, "NCAA: No Class At All."

Nebraska was playing the Seminoles on Saturday. But the opponent might as well have been the NCAA.

Three days before the game – the 1986 Nebraska season-opener – the NCAA informed Nebraska that 53 Huskers were suspended for one game and seven players for two. The crime: not following the "family, relatives or fellow students" rule on complimentary game passes.

The news hit like an earthquake around Lincoln and the state. Not only had Nebraska never been found guilty of an NCAA violation before, but here was trouble knocking at the door of the season-opener against the 11th-ranked Seminoles. NU officials, led by Nebraska coach Tom Osborne, were incensed. Not only had they felt lied to by NCAA investigators – who apparently had said that if Nebraska just came clean, nothing would happen – but they felt this was a ticky-tack violation at best. Players selling their complimentary tickets to make a buck? It happens everywhere, all the time. Didn't the NCAA have much bigger fish to fry?

Well, Nebraska's first victory of the 1986 season was getting a stay in the ruling, pending an appeal. All of the Huskers would be available against Florida State. Steve Taylor would suffice.

Taylor, a sophomore quarterback from San Diego, was the first "non-redshirt" sophomore to start a season at quarterback at Nebraska since Van Brownson in 1969. The anticipation over Taylor's debut was almost feverish around the state, much like when Turner Gill debuted in 1981 and, later, Tommie Frazier in 1992. And Taylor did not disappoint.

In the first night home game in Nebraska history, Taylor played like a veteran, showing poise and skill and a run-pass combination that would keep him under center for the next three seasons. This is where the Taylor Era started, under the lights, with the NCAA cloud hanging over the stadium, and Florida State up 17-10 early in the second half.

The Seminoles were becoming a little bothersome to the Nebraska program. Since agreeing to play in Lincoln four times in the 80s to build their program, the 'Noles were 2-1 against Nebraska, including a 17-13 win to open the 1985 season. And now here they were again, with running back Sammie Smith going 57 yards for a touchdown on a fake-reverse with 33 seconds left before halftime. And increasing it to 17-10 early in the third after a

Husker fumble.

Then it was Taylor time. And suddenly, everyone in the Red Palace forgot about the NCAA.

The 5-11, 195-pound Taylor led the Huskers on four consecutive scoring drives, starting with a 10-play, 63-yard drive capped by his six-yard touchdown run to tie the score with 5:15 left in the third quarter.

After an FSU punt, Taylor and the Huskers were moving again, this time 51 yards in six plays ending with a 12-yard touchdown pass from Taylor to tight end Todd Millikan.

By this time, the Blackshirts, led by senior middle guard Danny Noonan and sophomore linebacker Broderick Thomas, had put a clamp on FSU and quarterback Chip Ferguson. One of seven sacks of Ferguson forced another Seminole punt. And Taylor and the Huskers were off on a 67-yard, seven-play scoring drive that ended with a spectacular show of Taylor's big-play ability: a 46-yard touchdown pass to wingback Von Sheppard.

Another FSU punt. Another Taylor drive. This one ended in a 38-yard field goal by Dale Klein. No matter. Even Taylor's field goal drives were eating clock. This one took five minutes, 47 seconds.

With 1:23 left in the game, Nebraska was up 34-17. Just like that. The future had arrived. It wore No. 9.

"Steve Taylor played very, very well," Osborne said. "He has that kind of talent. You're always a little concerned in a first game against a tough oppponent on national TV. I think we're pretty good as long as we've got 'em all out there."

History shows that the Huskers would win the appeal and all 60 of the so-called culprits would be out there. More importantly, Taylor would be out there for three more seasons.

Red Zone

Neither rain nor NCAA suspensions could put a cloud over Husker fans' celebration of their team's 34-17 victory over FSU.

Nebraska quarterback Steve Taylor pitches to Keith Jones on a day to remember for Taylor: he completed 10 of 15 passes for 217 yards and five touchdowns to outduel UCLA's Troy Aikman.

Red Zone

Red Zone Game 33

Nebraska 42, UCLA 33
Sept. 12, 1987

LINCOLN – Let's see, now. If the Nebraska Cornhuskers couldn't run the option because their quarterback hurt a shoulder early in the game and had their lowest rushing total of the decade and coughed up four turnovers and all this came against a No. 3-ranked UCLA team with future NFL stars Troy Aikman, Ken Norton Jr., and James Washington, you would say:

A) The Huskers got smashed.

B) It was one of the great victories in Nebraska history.

Nebraska coach Tom Osborne chose (A).

"If somebody had told me we would only run for 117 yards and lose four fumbles, I'd have said we'd get whipped by 21 points," Osborne said.

Fortunately, Osborne was wrong. The No. 2-ranked Huskers showed why their early-season ranking was no joke by beating UCLA, 42-33, before a somewhat stunned, but gratified sellout crowd at Memorial Stadium.

Stunned, yes, because of the way the Huskers won the game: with a school record five touchdown passes. Who said Osborne was all scorched earth and wasn't hip to the ways of the left coast?

Not Steve Taylor. The Nebraska junior quarterback out-dueled Aikman on a day when the Huskers went to the air by necessity. He completed 10-of-15 passes (66.7 percent) for 217 yards and no interceptions. Taylor made his 10 completions count: half went for touchdowns, breaking the old Nebraska school mark of four held by Vince Ferragamo, Dave Humm and Turner Gill. Taylor tied the Big Eight mark held by former Kansas quarterback (and Oregon State basketball coach) Ralph Miller, who threw five TD passes against Washburn in 1938.

It started late in the first quarter when Taylor suffered a bruised left shoulder. The good news: Taylor is right-handed. The bad news: Taylor was done running options for the day. That would leave I-backs Ken Clark and Keith Jones slightly naked. But behind a bruising offensive line and a Blackshirt defense that held UCLA's Heisman Trophy candidate Gaston Green to 46 yards (stopping his string of 100-yard games at eight), the Huskers made do.

Having Dana Brinson around didn't hurt, either.

After UCLA took a quick 7-0 lead, Brinson, a wingback, sprinted Nebraska back into the game. Brinson returned the kickoff 47 yards and then caught passes for 14 and 24 yards. The touchdown pass, however, went to tight end Tom Banderas, from nine yards. After the Huskers got the ball back, Taylor threw an 11-yard touchdown pass to Clark, who had beaten Norton, for a 14-7 lead.

It was 14-10 Huskers minutes into the second half when the game turned. An Aikman fumble at his own 12 set up a Clark touchdown run. Then, after the Blackshirts held, Taylor hit a play-action pass to split end Rod Smith for a 48-yard touchdown that made it 28-10.

"I think it will shock the world that we had five touchdown passes," Smith said.

UCLA raced back with an Eric Ball touchdown that cut the lead to 28-17 with 3:11 left in the third quarter. But this was Taylor's game, Taylor's show. He led an eight-play, 74-yard drive aided by Taylor's 27-yard pass to Smith on third-and-nine. Then Taylor hit tight end Todd Milikan with a 35-yard touchdown pass with 14:54 to play.

Nine minutes later, Taylor had the record, and the Huskers had a 42-17 lead, with a 33-yard play-action pass to Millikan.

Meanwhile, the Blackshirts gave up a couple of late drives, and the Bruins got to within nine with 47 seconds left but they couldn't recover an onside kick.

"At halftime, we thought we had a chance," UCLA coach Terry Donahue said. "But the third quarter got away from us. When you don't generate enough yardage running, you get behind on down and distance. We put Nebraska in the same situation, but they were able to hit their play-action passes and we didn't execute as well."

Amazing, huh? The Monsters of the Midwest outpassed the West Coast Surfer Dudes. It was a wave the Huskers would ride all season to a No. 1 ranking and a "game of the century" showdown with Oklahoma later in the season. The Huskers had not only survived, they found a useful weapon in passing a very big test.

Red Zone

Red Zone Game 34

Nebraska 35, Oklahoma State 0
Oct. 17, 1987

STILLWATER, Okla. – Maybe Thurman Thomas should have just gotten some Juji Fruits.

But no, the Oklahoma State senior running back couldn't help himself the night before the 12th-ranked Cowboys were poised to play – and upset – the No. 2-ranked Nebraska Huskers at Lewis Field. This was the year. The Cowboys had their own version of the Triplets – Thomas, quarterback Mike Gundy and split end Hart Lee Dykes. They had Nebraska at home before a charged-up crowd of 50,440 at Lewis Field.

What they needed was a second movie theater in Stillwater.

It's tradition that college football teams see a movie the night before a game. It's not, however, commonplace for two teams to share the same theater complex and certainly not come out at the same time. But that's what happened on the eve of the Huskers' powerful and amazingly easy dismissal of the Cowboy threat, 35-0.

The teams were even leaving at the same time. What are the chances of that? What are the chances that Thomas would keep his mouth shut and not taunt the Husker defense? About as good as Oklahoma State beating the Huskers. And the two definitely were related.

"Thurman walked by and right in front of our whole defense, said, "You guys won't be able to stop me one-on-one,' Nebraska defensive end Broderick Thomas said. "It will take all 11 of you.

"He went off like the Tasmanian devil had jumped in his heart. I almost fell on the ground laughing."

B. Thomas would be laughing on Saturday but it was T. Thomas who would be on the ground. Thurman was right: it took 11 Huskers to bring him down. But he should have been more careful what he wished for.

Thomas, who entered the game leading the nation in rushing (140 yards per game) and a Heisman Trophy candidate, left with a 117.8 average and a Heisman concession speech after Nebraska had held him to seven yards in nine carries.

"That really pumped up the defense," said NU defensive tackle Neil Smith. "If we had lined up last night, it might have been worse than it turned out today."

It couldn't have been worse for Oklahoma State. The Pokes shot blanks all day. Sure, Gundy completed 20-of-42 passes for 221 yards but he was sacked four times and never got a sniff of the end zone. And Dykes, ranked sixth nationally in receiving, caught five passes for 113 yards, but TV replays showed Dykes might have gotten away with an offensive pass interference on a 47-yard catch. No matter. The Cowboys, the nation's fifth-highest scoring team, were shut out and held to 264 yards,

182 below their average.

It was a way-above-average game for the Blackshirts. Defensive coordinator Charlie McBride said it "was one of the better games we've played since I've been at Nebraska."

The Husker offense was almost an afterthought in this battle of the movie critics. I-backs Keith Jones and Ken Clark, both questionable earlier in the week with injuries, combined for 198 yards, in 30 carries, and four touchdowns. Quarterback Steve Taylor, who had missed the previous week with a bruised left shoulder, came back to throw for 140 yards and a touchdown.

But the story of the day was defense. Nebraska defense. McBride had thrown in a new twist, so to speak, by

having the ends and tackles loop around each other for an "inline stunt." It probably worked, but the Blackshirts were already so worked up that it probably wouldn't have mattered.

With Thomas bottled up, the Cowboys only ventured

The Huskers game at Oklahoma State in 1987 was a runaway, literally, for Steve Taylor and Co.

Red Zone

into scoring territory twice. The first trip ended in a Charles Fryar interception in the end zone. The other came late, at 35-0, when Gundy threw out of bounds on fourth down near the goal line. By then, a quiet, shifty back named Barry Sanders had replaced Thomas and wowed several Husker coaches and players with his breaktaking moves. The world would get introduced to Sanders, the OSU running back most likely to buy popcorn and shuffle quietly to his seat, in 1988.

"Where's Herschell?" asked NU coach Tom Osborne afterwards, feigning anger at Associated Press college football writer Herschell Nissenson picking the Cowboys for the upset. "Really, I felt the same way he did. I felt there was a good chance they could win the game."

Osborne must have seen the same movie Thomas did. Regardless, it was all pure fiction.

Oklahoma State's Thurman Thomas did all the pregame talking but Nebraska I-back Ken Clark (following John McCormick's block) did the running in Stillwater.

The Huskers shot out to a 42-0 second-quarter lead against Oklahoma State on moves like this from Steve Taylor.

Red Zone

Red Zone Game 35

Nebraska 63, Oklahoma State 42
Oct. 15, 1988

LINCOLN – Nebraska and Oklahoma State set out to play a football game on Oct. 15, 1988. But it was more like pinball.

The Huskers and Cowboys played a game that looked more futuristic than realistic. The sellout crowd at Memorial Stadium must have felt, at times, like it was watching a tennis match. Nebraska scored 63 points to Oklahoma State's rebuttal of 42 in a game that had the scoreboard flashing "Tilt" by game's end and had both defensive coordinators headed down to the local saloon where they could drown their sorrows in a pitcher of beer and flip to see who would play the first sad country song on the juke box.

On the other hand, this Nebraska victory was uplifting if you reveled in big plays and teams that scored before the cheerleaders could finish their push-ups in the end zone.

After seeing, but not necessarily believing, 1,117 total yards (662 by his own team) and a Memorial Stadium-record 105 points, Nebraska coach Tom Osborne wasn't sure what to think.

"This was like a 1983 game," Osborne said. "Those games were all 60-something or 70-something to 40. We have got to play better on defense."

Well, there were triplets on the field, but they belonged to Oklahoma State: quarterback Mike Gundy, split end

Hart Lee Dykes and running back Barry Sanders, whose 189 yards in 35 carries was the most for an opponent at Memorial Stadium since Penn State's Curt Warner ran for 238 yards in 1981. For Sanders, it was another brick in the wall of his Heisman Trophy-winning season, but it was overshadowed by Nebraska's own scoring explosion.

The Huskers had scored 63 points already that season – twice, against Utah State and the previous week at Kansas. But this was too much. Nebraska, led by senior I-back Ken Clark's 256 yards in 27 carries (the second-best in NU history behind Mike Rozier's 285 yards vs. Kansas in 1983) and three touchdowns, led 49-21 at halftime and 56-28 after three quarters. Senior quarterback Steve Taylor's day – three rushing TDs and two passing TDs (giving him a school career record 55) – were almost lost in the dust.

The Huskers thought they had it put away, early, too early, with a lightning-quick 42-0 lead with 11:42 left in the half.

But just as quickly, Sanders scored on consecutive possessions from nine and one yards, respectively. The Huskers then scored on a 10-play drive. And OSU took over with 1:50 left. But why run out the clock when you can just score? After a late hit on Gundy by Willie Griffin and Lawrence Pete that set up OSU at its 39, Gundy threw a bomb to Jarrod Green to the Nebraska 20. With three seconds left, Gundy found Dykes for a 12-yard touchdown that "cut" the lead to 49-21 at halftime.

Amazingly enough, the two defenses came back out for the second half.

Osborne, who said he didn't feel safe until an onside kick was recovered by NU with 1:33 left, was upset with his Blackshirts. But even he had to understand: It was natural for them to relax with such a big lead and Sanders, Dykes and Gundy weren't exactly chopped liver. The Cowboys' 455 total yards – 208 rushing and 247 passing – were more the rule than the exception that season.

"Oklahoma State can score on anybody," Osborne said. "But if we're going to have any chance to win the Big Eight championship, we have to stop people better than we did today."

Osborne would do well to write the day off as a freak of nature, a freak of a game no one would forget, except the two defensive coordinators crying in each other's beer.

Here's something you didn't always see in 1988: somebody lassoing Oklahoma State running back Barry Sanders. Here, it was Nebraska defensive end Broderick Thomas doing the honors.

Red Zone

Red Zone Game 36

Nebraska 7, Colorado 0
Nov. 12, 1988

LINCOLN – As those in another sellout crowd shuffled out of Memorial Stadium on a late-autumn Saturday, all they could do was shake their heads. There was no explanation whatsoever for Nebraska's 7-3 victory over Colorado.

The Husker defense, which had allowed over 40 points in two games already this season, finally got its first shutout – over a team averaging 27.7 points per game.

The Nebraska offense, averaging a nation-leading 46 points per game, was shut out for the first half for the second time this season and scored just once.

And then there was the heart-stopper of the day: Colorado running back J.J. Flannigan sprinting toward a sure Buffalo touchdown in the second quarter and mysteriously losing the ball and having to fall on it at his own 19.

No explanation.

"This is a funny team," Nebraska coach Tom Osborne said. "We think we've got a good offense. Our stats are very good. But we've had two games where we've been shut down pretty good. It's hard to figure."

There was this logic: The Buffs, under coach Bill McCartney, were starting to buy the Nebraska "rivalry" that McCartney was selling them. They played harder against Nebraska than anybody else. And, more importantly, McCartney's blue chips in recruiting were beginning to stack up. If nothing else on this day, the Buffs showed that they were creeping closer to Nebraska.

Still, that didn't explain why an above-average, hard-working CU defense could shut down a Big Red offense which had scored at least 47 points in seven different games in 1988. It was not exactly the kind of performance the seventh-ranked Huskers, 9-1, wanted heading into the next week's annual Oklahoma cage match.

Quarterback Steve Taylor's day was forgettable: 40 yards rushing and 2-of-9 passing for 18 yards. The Huskers were limited to 296 total yards – 205 in the second half, when they came alive for a brief moment.

That was in the third quarter, when Nebraska scored its lone touchdown. It was a 59-yard, nine-play drive that was more laborious than most. Senior I-back Ken Clark, who rushed for 165 yards on 28 carries (to move into fourth on Nebraska's single-season rushing chart with 1,330 yards), finished the drive with a two-yard run with 4:35 left in the third quarter. But only after Clark had dashed 10 yards on fourth-and-two at the CU 17.

With the offense out of it, the Blackshirts had to come up with some big plays and, in some cases, miracles.

The Buffs had three fumbles – all of which figured huge in the loss. One came in the second quarter when running back Eric Bieniemy was tackled after a 12-yard run deep inside Nebraska territory and NU free safety Tim Jackson came out of the pile holding the football. The officials ruled it was Nebraska's football. Then, with CU facing a crucial fourth-and-one at the Huskers' 27 in the fourth quarter, Buffs quarterback Sal Aunese fumbled the center snap and Flannigan recovered for a three-yard loss. Aunese later said the Nebraska crowd noise helped force the bad exchange.

But there was no plausible explanation for how Flannigan literally dropped the ball in the open field after bursting up the middle on a sprint draw in the second quarter.

"I was just trying to get a better grip on the ball," said Flannigan. "Once I put the move on the backer, I felt the ball slipping and I just tried to get a better grip on it. I saw the end zone and I guess I relaxed at the wrong time."

Indeed. A holding penalty and a reverse that was snuffed out for a 19-yard loss forced CU to punt. The reverse, to split end Jeff Campbell, was the same play that had burned NU defensive end Broderick Thomas two years earlier in a Nebraska loss at Colorado. This time, Thomas was ready and made the stop.

So preparation had something to do with it.

"The good Lord was looking over us on that one because he just flat dropped it," Nebraska defensive coordinator Charlie McBride said of Flannigan's fumble. "That, as it ends up, was really the game. So we were very, very fortunate."

That explanation was as good as any.

The Huskers and linebacker Leroy Etienne had their hands full with Colorado and Eric Bieniemy.

Red Zone

Tom Osborne consults with quarterback Steve Taylor during the Huskers' third-quarter scoring drive that proved crucial in a 7-3 win over Colorado.

On a freezing, sloppy day in Norman, Okla., Steve Taylor follows his blocking in for a one-yard touchdown run in the first quarter that amazingly held up to give the Huskers a 7-3 win and Big Eight championship.

Red Zone

Red Zone Game 37

Nebraska 7, Oklahoma 3
Nov. 19, 1988

NORMAN, Okla. – As Oklahoma quarterback Charles Thompson lay in a heap on the wet turf, with a chilled, driving rain falling down on his broken right leg, it was symbolic of the day for the Nebraska Cornhuskers.

They had come to Norman with a simple mission. They had come to break the Oklahoma stranglehold on the Big Eight championship, to break the Sooners' wishbone, their spirit, their fourth-quarter magic, any way they could.

There could not be another heartbreak for Steve Taylor, Broderick Thomas and Co. The Huskers had not beaten Oklahoma or won the Big Eight since 1983 and the Taylor-Thomas Era had witnessed the real nasty stuff. The fourth-quarter "Sooner Magic" comeback in 1986. Sooner domination in the No. 1 vs. No. 2 game in 1987. This game, played in an Oklahoma sleet under dark skies, was last call for the Taylor-Thomas era to get things done.

Which is why, as ugly as Nebraska's 7-3 victory in the muck was, it was that beautiful, too. If you looked hard enough through the driving sleet, you could actually see palm trees.

"Our players were really dedicated to this proposition all year long," Nebraska coach Tom Osborne said. "They really worked hard to be Big Eight champions."

Desire, indeed. The attitude was summarized in a letter that Taylor, the senior quarterback, had received before the game from his girlfriend.

"She said, "Steve, through all the struggles and media attack, and all the things you've gone through, nobody deserves it more than you,' Taylor said. "I read that over and over again.

"I was out there and I just thought about everything – two-a-days, and not winning and what the papers are going to say about us afterwards; I thought about all that stuff – my family, my career and what I want to do after this. I told myself I don't know if I can live with myself if I came to Nebraska and never beat OU."

That desire was obvious from the opening drive, into a biting 30 mile-an-hour wind. Taylor drove the Huskers 80 yards in nine plays. He bootlegged for nine yards on the first play. He hit Richard Bell with a 30-yard pass through the rain. He rolled right for 10 yards to the 1-yard line, where Taylor sneaked over for the touchdown with 11:06 left.

It would be Nebraska's only touchdown. The Huskers later squandered chances inside OU territory with penalties. They also had three turnovers.

But that touchdown would be all Nebraska needed.

Over on his side of the ball, Thomas was leading one of the great dominations in Blackshirt history. The tall, brash and loud Thomas knew this was a day for actions, not words. Nebraska's defense was all about action: the Blackshirts snapped the wishbone into pieces, a wishbone that had been averaging 438 yards per game. But in this rain, this Black rain,– Oklahoma was held to 137 total yards – the lowest Sooner total against Nebraska in the Devaney-Osborne era – and just 98 yards rushing, the lowest total since the wishbone had been installed in 1970. Only once did Oklahoma penetrate the Huskers' 25-yard line. That came in the third quarter, when the Sooners scored their only points on a R.D. Lashar field goal from 29 yards.

That was due, in large part, to a new wrinkle on defense that the Husker staff had taken from the Miami Hurricanes' attacking 4-3 defense. Osborne described the defense as "a little like a 4-3 with a middle linebacker." The Nebraska staff had seen Miami stuff the Sooners with it in the previous year's Orange Bowl and decided to try it. But this day was more than about schemes. It was about heart and desire and character.

"There has been a lot of talk about Oklahoma "magic,' the fourth quarter and choking and all of that," Osborne said. "But we talked a lot today about how we would play in the fourth quarter."

Magnificently. Bravely. OU had one last gasp. The Sooners took over on the Nebraska 48 with 1:45 to play.

But three straight plays, including two incompletions by Thompson, got nowhere. Finally, on fourth down, Willie Griffin and Lawrence Pete sandwiched the little Sooner quarterback – the same one who had pranced into Lincoln the year before and broken so many hearts.

It was nothing personal against Thompson, said Thomas, who said he hoped the quarterback was okay. Thomas sat in the interview room, wearing a small clock on a chain around his neck. Why?

"This means it was time for a new Big Eight champion," Thomas said.

Just in time.

Red Zone

Nebraska defensive tackle Willie Griffin stands over Oklahoma quarterback Charles Thompson on one of the Blackshirts' finest days.

Coach Tom Osborne seeks an explanation on a second-quarter call. Tom Osborne made Husker history by starting true freshman quarterback Tommie Frazier at Missouri.

Red Zone Game 38

Nebraska 34, Missouri 24
Oct. 24, 1992

COLUMBIA, Mo. – A group of Nebraska writers was sitting around a hotel bar on the Friday night before the Huskers' game at Missouri in 1992. One of the writers in the group, *World-Herald* Nebraska beat writer Lee Barfknecht, was missing. He had heard a tip that Nebraska coach Tom Osborne was going to start Tommie Frazier on Saturday. Freshman Tommie Frazier. He would be the first true freshman ever to start a game at quarterback for Nebraska.

This was history. This was news. Finally, Lee joined our group. He had called the Nebraska team hotel and reached Osborne's room to ask him about the tip.

"He said he hadn't decided yet," Lee B. said.

Such was the espionage surrounding Frazier's debut as a Husker. The highly-sought, much-celebrated freshman from Florida was seen as a sort of savior who could take Nebraska back to the top. Osborne had made the decision on Thursday night: He would start Frazier. Senior Mike Grant had a stiff back. But this was a handy time to do it because Grant also was struggling to move the offense. And the offense, the program, needed a shot of adrenaline.

On Oct. 22, 1992, that shot was delivered. The Frazier Era, one of the most magnificent in NU history, had begun. Nebraska beat Missouri, 34-24, to set up a Big

Eight title collision with Colorado the next week in Lincoln. And the Huskers couldn't have done it without Frazier. Already, the comparisons to former NU great Turner Gill, now his position coach, were starting.

"At this age, Tommie Frazier is in the Turner Gill category," said Nebraska defensive coordinator Charlie McBride. "He showed a lot of poise. He showed the look of a winner."

Frazier, a poised option-maker with an erratic arm, was most dangerous in one category: making plays. He showed that all afternoon, as his No. 15 was unveiled to the world of Big Red. Frazier scored on runs of seven and three yards to give NU a 14-0 lead after the first quarter. When Missouri tied the game at 14, Frazier led two second-quarter scoring drives for a 24-14 halftime lead.

As the Blackshirts were being scorched for 424 yards and two touchdowns by MU's Jeff Handy – not a good sign for the Colorado game – none of the 12,000 red-clad Husker fans at Faurot Field seemed to care. They were mesmerized by Frazier, who rushed for 77 yards and three touchdowns and completed 9-of-20 passes for 157 yards. But, more than stats, the thing about Frazier was that good things – big plays – seemed to happen around him.

The Huskers' second scoring drive was a classic example. Frazier had an 18-yard screen pass to I-back Calvin Jones.

He pump-faked away a pass rusher and threw a 43-yard pass to wingback Vincent Hawkins, who made a diving catch at the 11 (some fans wondered if the Huskers would attempt diving catches for anyone else). Then Frazier went the final seven yards on an option.

But it was one run in particular that stuck in everyone's mind that day. It was like shooting a starter's pistol that the Frazier era was now off and running. It came with NU clinging to a 27-24 lead entering the fourth quarter. The Huskers had fourth-and-goal at the Missouri 5-yard line. Osborne said go for it. And Frazier did.

He rolled right, kept and appeared bogged down. But then Frazier took off like a long jumper at about the three and landed shoulder-first over a pile of players into the end zone. Who was this guy? Superman?

"If we had kicked the field goal, we would've been up by six," Osborne said. "That's nice, but the way they moved the ball on us at times, we weren't sure we wouldn't get beat by a point.

"So we went for it. We just put it in his hands to make a play. And he made a tremendous play."

Frazier had only just begun to play.

Red Zone

Husker I-back Calvin Jones leaps over a pile of Tigers.

Colorado freshman quarterback Koy Detmer is given an old-fashioned welcome to Nebraska by Trev Alberts (34) and John Parrella (92).

Red Zone Game 39

Nebraska 52, Colorado 7
Oct. 31, 1992

LINCOLN – Blood is thicker than Kool-Aid.

That was the unmistakable message on Halloween Day, 1992, at Memorial Stadium. Colorado and Nebraska, both ranked eighth in the country, played a game that would be for bragging rights, psychological turf, pole position for the Big Eight Conference title and, more importantly, the manhood of every Nebraska football player dressed in red.

Blood red.

It was that kind of day, on a Dark Shadows kind of day, with the dark clouds hanging eerily low over Memorial Stadium like something out out a monster movie. But the scariest sights were in black and gold. Colorado had targeted Nebraska as its rival, then the Buffs had the audacity to win two straight games and Big Eight titles from the Huskers, tie for a third in 1991 and now, with the Colorado media and fans awash in name-calling and Husker-joking, it was time for the Huskers to take a stand.

The Buffs were terminally-hip with their technologically-sound one-back offense, the wave of the future. The Huskers were the prehistoric farm boys whose timeless running offense was about to grind to a halt in the 90s. Except everyone forgot one thing.

Blood is thicker than Kool-Aid.

"You line up against a guy and you beat him or he beats you," Nebraska defensive tackle John Parrella said. "There's no stalemate. Your heart is either beating blood or Kool-Aid."

The Huskers scored 52 points and proved many more in beating CU, 52-7. Of utmost significance was the fact that the Huskers won "a big one." Having not won a Big Eight title or beaten a top-10 team since 1988, and having lost five straight bowls, the Nebraska program needed a statement game.

Those statements came early and often. The Huskers, who moved to 6-1 and 3-0, were on Colorado from the first play – an interception by NU linebacker Travis Hill. They built a 17-0 lead and increased it to 24-7. In the second half, it was all trick-or-treat for the Huskers. The Colorado offense was in their sack.

Which is what Nebraska coaches had hoped. They knew the CU offense, led by sophomore quarterback Kordell Stewart, lived off of big plays. So they were going to make the Buffs drive on them. They blitzed rarely and had the secondary drop back to the State Capitol. Why? Because the Buffs would be starting true freshman quarterback Koy Detmer, who had great promise but had also thrown five interceptions in his first start two weeks ago, against Oklahoma. And because the Buffs had neither the strong offensive line nor the running game –

ala Miami or Washington – to outmuscle the Huskers. Osborne felt he could turn Hill, Parrella and Trev Alberts loose and things would work out.

All the Blackshirts did was produce six turnovers – three fumble recoveries and three interceptions– and sack Detmer three times. The young quarterback spent most of the time running for his life. Detmer was 9-of-26 passing for 119 yards while big-play receivers Charles Johnson and Michael Westbrook combined for just five catches. Meanwhile, Stewart entered the game late in the third quarter, but completed just three passes for 17 yards and was sacked twice.

The signature play of the day, and also the biggest, came with CU taking over at its 44 with 1:49 left in the first half. The Buffs trailed, 17-7, but they had just scored, using a no-huddle offense, and had some momentum.

It didn't last long. On first down, Hill beat his man, slapped the ball out of Detmer's exposed hand and recovered it. Nebraska used the turnover to build a 24-7 lead.

There were other big plays. Tommie Frazier, in only his second start, threw two touchdown passes and the Huskers rushed for five more, including an electric 47-yard sprint by junior I-back Calvin Jones through a huge hole on the left side on a counter sweep. Jones took his helmet off in the end zone in celebration. The fans were jumping up and down and screaming. It was an emotional day, one of equal joy and relief.

"We wanted this one bad," Hill said. "I've had a taste in my mouth since 1989."

It was the taste of blood, not Kool-Aid.

Red Zone

With moves like this, it's no wonder Nebraska offensive guard Will Shields won the Outland Trophy in 1992. Here, Shields takes on CU's Chris Hudson (47) and Leonard Renfro on a 16-yard fumbleroosky run.

Red Zone Game 40

Nebraska 14, UCLA 13
Sept. 18, 1993

PASADENA, Calif. – Before he became Lawrence Phillips, controversial figure and the bane of media and women's rights groups nationwide, Lawrence Phillips was just another quiet kid on the Nebraska bench.

But all that changed on Sept. 18, 1993.

That was the day the eighth-ranked Huskers went out to the West Coast and found themselves in quick need of a lifeguard. Nebraska was without its top I-back, Calvin Jones, and backup Damon Benning was fumbling and unranked UCLA, playing at home in the Rose Bowl, had an early 10-0 lead. Suddenly, the picture-postcard mountains around the historic Rose Bowl were closing in fast on Nebraska. The Huskers needed a hero.

They found an unexpected one in Phillips.

Phillips was a true freshman that year, a kid, basically, fresh from the mean streets of L.A. with a troubled past that landed him in a boys home. For all the problems he would later have at Nebraska, the day he led the Huskers to a comeback 14-13 victory over UCLA was one of his finer moments.

Phillips, whose home was 30 minutes from the Rose Bowl, rushed for 137 yards on 28 carries and scored on a five-yard run. It was the kind of steady performance the Huskers needed to fall back on until they could get their new 4-3 defense set.

Indeed, it was still early in the transition process for the Blackshirts, who had moved from the 5-2 to the attacking 4-3 scheme fulltime in 1993. That meant there would be busts. UCLA took advantage of some early. The Bruins built a 10-0 lead in the second quarter on a 39-yard field goal by freshman Bjorn Merten and a 72-yard drive capped by a six-yard touchdown run by freshman Skip Hicks.

But it could have been much worse. The Huskers were dodging bullets all day. UCLA recovered three Husker fumbles and intercepted a Tommie Frazier pass but could not convert any of the turnovers into points. Also, Hicks had a first-quarter 53-yard touchdown run called back by a holding penalty and Merten missed field goal tries of 53 and 44 yards.

"It wasn't pretty at all," said NU outside linebacker Trev Alberts, whose 10 solo tackles earned him ABC-TV's Nebraska player-of-the-game honors. "But I'm going back to Lincoln with a smile on my face. We beat a very tough team in a hostile situation. This will pay big dividends."

For one, it kept an 11-0 regular-season alive and well. And the Huskers found a new offensive threat. With Jones out with a knee strain suffered in the season-opener, and Benning benched after two early fumbles, coach Tom Osborne inserted Phillips to see if he could provide a spark. He would, scoring on a five-yard sweep with 2:54

left in the first half to get NU on the board.

Later, Phillips ran 29 yards on five carries to set up the go-ahead touchdown – an 11-yard pass from Frazier to tight end Gerald Armstrong with 6:56 left in the third quarter.

UCLA would get another field goal but that was as close as the Bruins got. The Nebraska offense was staying on the field longer, thanks to Phillips, who accounted for 92 of NU's 185 yards in the second half. Phillips, playing before 20-30 friends and family in his second college game, relished the moment.

"To go over 100 yards for the first time and do it back home, that's special," Phillips said. "I may never get a chance to play in California again, so I'm definitely going to remember this."

It was a Phillips moment to remember.

Red Zone Game 41

Nebraska 17, Kansas State 6
Oct. 15, 1994

MANHATTAN, Kan. – "Nebraska is still Nebraska. Kansas State is still Kansas State."

That memorable quote, from the lips of Nebraska linebacker Ed Stewart, was the bottom line in the aftermath of NU's 17-6 win, one of the most improbable Husker victories ever, a braveheart of a game that made legends out of almost every Husker who was involved.

Driving to the game that Saturday morning, you understood this was no ordinary trip to tiny, unassuming KSU Stadium for a typical 59-7 Husker win. At 8:30 a.m. – three hours before kickoff – the streets around KSU Stadium were jammed, the parking lots packed with cars and clouded with tailgate-grill smoke and the purple Wildcat flags flapping in the wind. Some 1,000 extra folding chairs were set out for an overflow crowd.

They had come to see history: the end of the Wildcats' 25-year losing streak to Nebraska and the beginning of a K-State era atop the Big Eight and in the Orange Bowl. Oh, this was the year. Just ask the Wildcats. Led by quarterback Chad May, who had thrown for 489 yards against NU in 1993, they were bubbling with overconfidence and their quotes filled the newspapers – and Husker locker room.

The Wildcat bravado was based on two things 1) they felt they could pass on Nebraska and 2) the Huskers were without quarterback Tommie Frazier, who was suffering from blood clots in his leg. But not only was Frazier out, his backup, Brook Berringer, was questionable with a collapsed lung. That meant diminutive walk-on, Matt Turman, would get the start.

But the plan was flawed. The Wildcats underestimated two things: 1) the size of the Huskers' hearts and 2) the fast maturity of a 4-3 defense that was built to muffle these newfangled one-back offenses.

It was that defense that owned the day, holding Kansas State to 242 yards – 105 below its average – and 62 of that came on the Wildcats' only scoring drive, capped with an electrifying 29-yard touchdown pass from May to Mitch Running on the first play of the second quarter. But no sooner was the crowd up than it was silenced: NU linebacker Troy Dumas blocked the extra point and Nebraska still led, 7-6.

Dumas later picked off a pass, breaking May's Big Eight-record string of consecutive passes thrown during regular-season play without an interception at 148. Amazingly, the Huskers held down May while playing mostly man-to-man – the same coverage May predicted he would thrive in. All the Blackshirts did was drop Stewart or Dumas back into the combination zone-man coverage.

But it was mostly guts, not schemes, that held down the

fort for Nebraska, especially in the first half, with Nebraska's offense sputtering. Kansas State moved into NU territory on four of six first-half possessions. Typical was a 16-play, 6 1/2-minute drive that ended in Martin Gramatica's missing a 37-yard field goal.

That kind of breathing room was what Turman, Berringer and Lawrence Phillips needed. It's amazing how they scored 17 points.

Consider that when Turman was in the game, the Wildcats knew the Huskers wouldn't pass. And when Berringer was in the game, there would be no options. NU went mostly with straight, basic, power football. But even that wasn't easy, not with Phillips running with a painful thumb injury.

L.P. may have had more prolific rushing days, but not a better day as a running back than this one. On NU's opening drive, starting at the K-State 28 after a muffed punt, Phillips was the only ball carrier, covering all 28 yards in six hard-nosed, vanilla plays. The Wildcats knew where the ball was going, but their nine-man front still couldn't stop Phillips, who had 117 yards in 31 carries, many of which came in the second half after Phillips had gone to a local hospital to have his left thumb numbed.

Berringer was just as gutsy, playing briefly in the second quarter before taking over late in the third for good. The junior from Goodland, Kan., led an 11-play 75-yard scoring drive that had K-State off-balance. After Phillips ran 17 yards, Berringer went to fullback Jeff Makovicka

for a 15-yard touchdown with 11:01 to play. Darin Erstad added a 24-yard field goal with 1:32 to play and the tailgate fires were out.

Inside the Wildcat interview room, May was talking softly and nursing a poked eye, courtesy of NU defensive tackle Christian Peter, who added injury to insult, though it was the Huskers who had felt the most insulted.

"To them, they were all this and that and we were supposed to be nothing," Stewart said. "We didn't have Tommie Frazier, so supposedly we were inferior. What do they say now?"

That it was one of the most incredible victories in Nebraska history.

This play summarized Colorado quarterback Kordell Stewart's day against Nebraska (and linebacker Dwayne Harris) in 1994.

Red Zone

Red Zone Game 42

Nebraska 24, Colorado 7
Oct. 29, 1994

LINCOLN – Before his young life was tragically taken in a plane crash in the spring of 1996, Brook Berringer left behind many fond memories for Nebraska fans.

This one may stand out the most.

Berringer, who represented the quiet, hard-working Nebraska player who waited his turn in the shadows of the Husker program, finally got his chance on Oct. 29, 1994. Berringer, a tall, dark junior with movie star looks, was an unlikely candidate for hero that day. The Goodland, Kan., kid had only made a handful of starts, in the absence of Tommie Frazier, and here he was, with No.3 Nebraska taking on No. 2 Colorado – and a home underdog to boot – with Heisman Trophy candidate Rashaan Salaam and the ever-dangerous Buff offense rolling into Memorial Stadium.

Colorado coach Bill McCartney had tried to plant seeds of doubt in Berringer's head during the week, wondering aloud how Berringer would handle the pressure. But that was a question on every Husker fan's mind. They hardly knew Brook. But they would love what they found.

Nebraska beat, no, dominated Colorado, 24-7, to stake its claim for the No. 1 ranking. And the difference was Berringer.

His cool, collected play gave the Huskers an anchor in the biggest game of the season. Berringer completed 12-of-17 passes for 142 yards, with a touchdown and

interception, and rushed seven times for 19 yards. But it wasn't the numbers. Berringer led the Huskers to scores on four of their first six drives. It was magical, the way he took over, assumed the leadership role, got the crowd up, put everyone at ease, like he had been doing it all his life. It was like watching Al Pacino transform himself by the end of the first "Godfather" movie.

The best thing Berringer did was make coach Tom Osborne's game plan work. Osborne had several new wrinkles up his sleeve for the Buffs, things he'd never shown. The biggest was a pass to the tight end. Nebraska? Throw? The NU staff had seen the Colorado linebackers on film and how they always were quick to support the run. Osborne had Berringer play-action pass over and over and the Buff linebackers, on cue, bit on the run. That meant tight ends Mark Gilman and Eric Alford were constantly open. Nine of Berringer's 12 completions went to the tight ends, with Alford catching five passes for 78 yards and a 30-yard touchdown pass in the third quarter. Alford and Gilman accounted for 46 of 73 yards on a scoring drive late in the first half that gave NU its 17-0 halftime lead.

It may as well have been Berringer 17, Colorado 0. His presence was that powerful.

"Brook was great," Osborne said. "It was just like he was going out for a scrimmage. He didn't show any wear or tear. You'd think a guy in that situation might. Kansas

State was a big game, but he didn't start that one. So this was the biggest game he had ever been involved in and he responded well."

Much better than Kordell Stewart, the Buffs' quarterback who was so brilliant 10 games a year and so helpless against Nebraska. Stewart completed 12-of-28 passes for 150 yards and none of it mattered. Worse, Stewart couldn't run (seven yards total) and that meant the Buffs were doomed against NU's blitzing defense. Especially Salaam, who rushed 22 times for a rather meaningless 134 yards. The Husker defensive coaches had a simple strategy: focus on Salaam, especially on the option, and make Stewart beat them.

History said he couldn't. Stewart seemed helpless, locked-up, against Nebraska. History was right again. Twice in the third quarter, with the Buffs at the NU 35 and 24, Stewart was tackled for a loss on third down to halt the drive.

Now Nebraska was 9-0 and 4-0 and driving toward a date in the Orange Bowl for the national title. With a guy named Berringer – whom everyone now knew – behind the wheel.

"I went into this game and totally blocked it out," said Berringer of the flak jacket he wore to protect a lung that had collapsed earlier in the season. "It felt good. I felt like we had them on their heels the whole time. Anytime you've got your whole

scheme of things going, it's a big help."

Berringer was the biggest help and Nebraska would never forget it.

Cory Schlesinger breaks past Colorado for a 14 yard touchdown run. Schlesinger finished with 65 yards on eight carries.

Red Zone

Who said Colorado wasn't a rival? Husker fans let down their guard, and the goalpost, after thumping Colorado, 24-7, in 1994.

Maybe the turning point of the 1995 Orange Bowl: the Huskers' Dwayne Harris sacks Miami quarterback Frank Costa in the end zone for a third-quarter safety.

Red Zone Game 43

Nebraska 24, Miami, Fla. 17 (Orange Bowl)
Jan. 1, 1995

MIAMI, Fla. – Joe Paterno was right.

Nebraska coach Tom Osborne won his first national championship when he least expected it. And where he least expected it.

In the east end zone of the Orange Bowl.

It was there, on a starry, starry night in south Florida, that Osborne exorcised his demons in this classic old football stadium, which had teased and taunted him over the year. And Osborne did it in the east end zone, where the ghosts of his past lived all these years.

There, where Turner Gill's two-point conversion pass fell to the ground against Miami in 1984, quarterback Tommie Frazier hit tight end Eric Alford with a two-point conversion pass that tied the 1995 Orange Bowl with Miami at 17 with 7:38 to play.

There, in the end zone where Byron Bennett's long field goal try went left against Florida State in the previous year's Orange Bowl, Nebraska scored twice up the middle. There, where FSU's William Floyd appeared to fumble before scoring a controversial touchdown in the 1994 game, Nebraska fullback Cory Schlesinger twice went in untouched.

This time, Nebraska won the Orange Bowl and the national championship all at once, 24-17, over the dreaded Hurricanes.

True, this wasn't your older brother's Miami. The Canes had an average quarterback (by their standards) in Frank Costa and were looking more vulnerable by the year. But they still were playing in their backyard alley, the Orange Bowl, where they had a partisan crowd waving those orange-and-green Hurricane flags and where they had won 62 of their last 63 games.

It still was a house of horrors for Osborne, a bowl game and stadium with almost a life of its own as the old coach's nemesis.

And now Osborne, who says he loves to coach for the challenge, the chess game, had a doozy. Osborne would have to make several key decisions to win this game. It was almost as if the Orange Bowl were challenging him to answer a riddle, like the great Sphinx, before entering.

Who to start at quarterback? Frazier, his play-making winner, hadn't played in months. Brook Berringer had stepped in admirably in Frazier's place and gotten the Huskers this far. Osborne rolled the dice and chose Frazier.

How long do you stay with Tommie? Osborne had a plan to alternate quarterbacks to keep Miami's defense off-balance. Frazier played the first quarter, Berringer the second. Miami led 10-7 at the half and 17-7 late in the third quarter. Osborne stuck with Berringer. For now.

Pass or run? After his superbly-built defense paid a dividend by sacking Costa for a safety, Nebraska got a break: an illegal kick by Miami set up NU at the Hurricanes' 4 just as the fourth quarter began. But rather than try to ram it in over Warren Sapp and Co., Osborne had Berringer pass. The quarterback's toss to Alford in the end zone was intercepted by leaping safety Earl Little.

So maybe Osborne was trying too hard, trying to outsmart the Sphinx. But the Sphinx was in a generous mood. He gave Osborne one more shot.

Final question: Berringer or Frazier? Pass or option game with Nebraska down, 17-9?

Tommie. The rest is history. Husker history.

"I just felt like it was time for Tommie," Osborne said. "It was a gut feeling. I was prepared to go the rest of the game with Brook. But Tommie had fresh legs."

Indeed. The Huskers went 40 yards in two plays and 59 yards in in seven plays to tie the game and take a seven-point lead. All in the fourth quarter. All in the east end zone. The difference was Frazier's options against the now-fatigued Hurricane defense. Just ask the portly Sapp, who, when Frazier had re-entered the game, had cracked, "Hey, Tommie, where you been?"

"It's not where I've been, fat boy," Frazier said in reply, "It's where I'm going."

Nebraska was going to the top. Finally. The pollsters gave Osborne both Associated Press and USA Today/CNN championship blessings the next day, leaving undefeated and Rose Bowl champion Penn State on the outside at No. 2. Justice? Perhaps. Husker fans still recalled vividly the controversial 1982 game at Penn State that knocked NU out of the national title.

Either way, Osborne would not campaign openly, as his predecessor, Bob Devaney, had done 15 years earlier with his "Even the Pope would vote us No. 1" quote.

"I told Joe Paterno I wouldn't do any lobbying and I'm not going to," Osborne said. "I don't think Joe will, either. If they give it to us, we'll be very grateful and certainly take it home. If they don't, I'll understand that, too. But I'll always be proud of the way we played."

This time, Osborne got the inner satisfaction, the irony, the justice and, finally, the trophy.

Cory Schlesinger, the late-game hero of the 1995 Orange Bowl, puts the finishing touch on Tom Osborne's first national championship.

Finally, the Miami dragon was dead. And the Huskers were champs!

Red Zone

Typically, everyone around Tom Osborne shows emotion – except Osborne – in the biggest moment of his career. But there's probably still one more play to coach.

Vintage Tommie Frazier: in the biggest game of the 1995 season, at Colorado, Touchdown Tommie (here running through CU's Matt Russell) had the game of his career.

Red Zone

Red Zone Game 44

Nebraska 44, Colorado 21
Oct. 28, 1995

BOULDER, Colo. – His teams won four Big Eight championships and two national championships. There was the trip to the Downtown Athletic Club, the comeback from blood clots, the 75-yard run in the Fiesta Bowl that became legend and a poster, in that order.

But, in this author's mind, one image of Tommie Frazier will always stand out above others. One game defined Frazier's career and one play in that game (and not the run in the Fiesta Bowl) defined what No. 15 was all about.

The game was Nebraska's 44-21 victory at Colorado in 1995.

The play came midway through the second quarter, with Nebraska ahead, 21-14 and NU with first down at the Buffs' 42. One unbelievable, unforgettable, totally Tommie-like play.

Frazier dropped back to pass. Tight end Mark Gilman was open deep. But then, suddenly, Colorado defensive end Mike Phillips blindsided Frazier, helmet-first, chest-high.

Down goes Frazier? No. Not yet. Frazier absorbed the hit – one that would have sent many other quarterbacks to the turf – and held onto the ball. And with Phillips pulling him down, Frazier managed to get his right arm free enough to flick a pass out to I-back Ahman Green on the sidelines for a 35-yard gain to the 7-yard line.

Nebraska would only get a field goal out of the play, but the psychological damage had been done. The message: you could hit Frazier as hard as you wanted. He wasn't going down. He would not be denied.

The ones who saw it couldn't believe it and the ones who didn't could.

"It was absolutely phenomenal," said Husker outside linebackers coach Tony Samuel, who watched it from the coaches' booth in the press box. "That was as great a play as I've ever seen. It's unbelieveable."

"He's a tough guy," said wingback Jon Vedral. "I didn't see it, but if someone tells me something like that about Tommie, I believe it."

This was one of the tougher assignments in the Frazier Era (1992-95). Second-ranked Nebraska at seventh-ranked Colorado in front of a record 54,023 at Folsom Field. The Buffs had a top-10 offense, led by hot backup quarterback John Hessler, and a team full of veterans who had lost three straight to NU. Nebraska would have to play a near-perfect game to win.

How would a perfect game do?

The Huskers had no penalties, no turnovers, allowed no sacks, had a balanced offense (226 yards rushing and 241 passing), held CU to 20 points and 122 yards under its average and scored on the first play of the game – a play designed to score by Osborne – when Ahman Green took a pitch left, broke to the sidelines and sprinted 57 yards. They even got the perfect pre-game speech. After the Buffs had gone through some ridiculous pre-game ritual of a big Samoan beating a war drum and the players leading the crowd in "War Time! War Time!" Osborne told his team, "Teams that do that are worried and are looking for something to help them."

That was first-year Buff coach Rick Nueheisel's first Nebraska game. He didn't know it would take more than a war drum to beat Frazier.

The senior had his best game, in more ways than one. He completed a career-high 14-of-23 passes for a career-high 241 yards and two touchdowns. His 52-yard touchdown bomb to Clester Johnson put NU ahead 21-7. His seven-yard touchdown pass to Vedral with 10 seconds left in the half gave NU a deflating 31-14 lead. Not bad for a guy who can't pass.

But, as usual with Frazier, it was the little things that made the difference. One big reason the Huskers had no penalties was that Frazier was totally cool under the thunderclap of Folsom Field crowd noise, particularly late in the second half on an 83-yard scoring drive when Frazier called audibles by tapping his helmet. The Buffs were counting on some illegal procedure penalties and got none. They overplayed the run to make Frazier pass and were counting on that, too. Wrong again.

"He shocked us," CU's Phillips said. "We never thought he could come out and rip us apart like he did. He came up big for them."

But didn't he always? If you hadn't learned that by this game, you never would.

Red Zone Game 45

Nebraska 62, Florida 24 (Fiesta Bowl)
Jan. 2, 1996

TEMPE, Ariz. – I'll never forget the morning after the 1996 Fiesta Bowl. It was just before 8 a.m. in a ballroom at the Mission Palms Hotel in downtown Tempe, just down the street from where Nebraska had beaten Florida, 62-24, the night before for the national championship. In the room that morning were Nebraska writers, radio and TV guys and a handful of national college writers. All waiting for Nebraska coach Tom Osborne to enter the room and talk about his second straight national championship.

When he arrived, most of the reporters' eyes got wide.

Osborne looked terrible. He looked beaten down, his face wrinkled and his eyes red and tired. For the first time in a long time, Osborne looked old. He was tired. But not from a long night. From a long season.

The 1995 season had been Osborne's longest season. It centered on an incident in September, when his star I-back, junior Lawrence Phillips, had beaten his ex-girlfriend. Suddenly, a handful of unrelated incidents involving NU players over the last few years got lumped in by the national media. Osborne was bashed in every corner of the country. Months after being glorified after his first national title, Osborne was now a "win at all costs" coach for bringing Phillips back onto the team. CBS sent a reporter to ambush him at a press conference. The Huskers were 12-0. But Osborne couldn't win.

Worse, he couldn't enjoy his team's remarkable growth and accomplishments.

Quietly, and privately, though, Osborne must have loved his team's total demolition of Florida.

Few gave Nebraska a chance to win, even though the Huskers were ranked No. 1 and the Gators No. 2. But Florida coach Steve Spurrier was the resident genius of the hour in college football. And even though NU's defense had proven it could stop Miami and Colorado, nobody thought the Blackshirts would stop Florida's "Fun n' Gun" offense and quarterback Danny Wuerffel.

They didn't, early. Florida led 3-0 and 10-6 in the first quarter with Wuerffel completing short passes down the field. But after a 42-yard touchdown run by Phillips, making his first start since the second game of the season, the game turned dramatically.

With Florida starting on its eight-yard line, the Blackshirts took over. It was for a moment like this that Osborne decided to switch to the 4-3 defense back in 1992. Weakside linebacker Terrell Farley – small and fast enough to be a safety in most defenses – sacked Wuerffel for a seven-yard loss. Then, on second-and-31, with Florida using five wide receivers and nobody in the backfield to block, NU linebacker Jamel Williams – another smallish linebacker – raced in untouched and sacked

Wuerffel for a safety.

After the free kick, quarterback Tommie Frazier and I-back Ahman Green helped the Huskers score in seven plays for a 22-10 lead with 9:13 left in the second quarter.

That sequence was basically the game. If Wuerffel wasn't rattled then, an interception by Michael Booker and 42-yard return for touchdown should have done the job. Nebraska led 35-10 at the half and it was over. Not only couldn't Florida move the ball on NU's zone coverage, but the Gators had no shot against Nebraska's bullish offensive line and running backs.

Did Phillips help? Sure, his presence set a physical tone, especially early when he broke for a 23-yard run and a 42-yard touchdown and he whistled by everyone on a 16-yard touchdown pass from Frazier. But on this night the Huskers could have won big without Phillips.

"This isn't a surprise," said center Aaron Graham. "After watching film, we knew we could move the ball on them. We thought it would be a four-quarter game. But Florida started to wear down physically in the first half. It got to the point where we had plays that we thought were automatic touchdowns."

The lopsidedness of the game was illustrated on the game's signature play: a 75-yard touchdown run by Frazier in the fourth quarter in which seven Florida defenders had a hand on Frazier (sometimes three at a time) and Frazier still broke free. Frazier, who had a career-high 199 yards in rushing and two touchdowns, was named MVP for the third straight bowl game. Nebraska set school records for most points, rushing yards (524) and total yards (629) in a bowl. Several wags in the press box were writing that Nebraska's 1995 edition was "the greatest team in college football history," a title once given to the 1983 and 1971 Huskers.

What the Huskers had done was methodically go about repeating as national champions (the first consensus repeat champs since Oklahoma in 1955-56) with hard work and poise – in the face of great scrutiny and adversity. For that, Osborne had to feel gratitude and pride. But that would take time.

"This has been a terrible year and a great year," Osborne said the next morning, and by the look on his face, everyone believed him.

Red Zone

Florida quarterback Danny Wuerffel gets sacked by Jamel Williams for a second-quarter safety and begins to get a taste for what is yet to come.

Touchdown Tommie Frazier is No. 1. And so are the Huskers, for the second straight year.

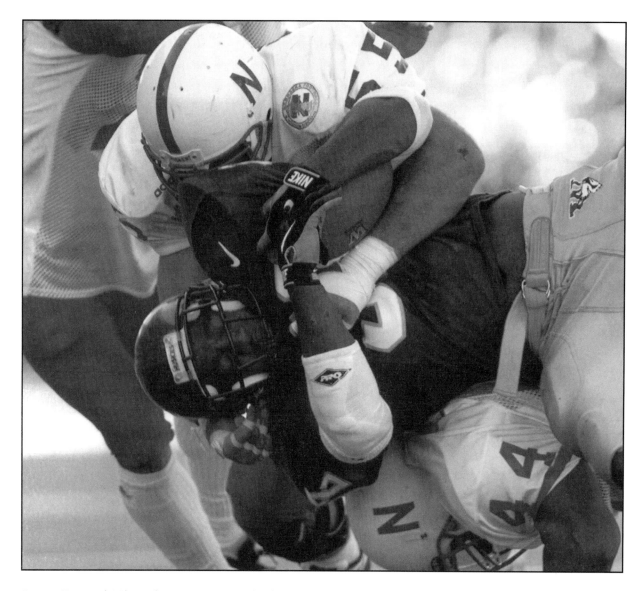

Jason Peter (55) and Jay Foreman (44) swarm Washington tailback Maurice Shaw late in the Huskers' victory.

Red Zone Game 46

Nebraska 27, Washington 14
Sept. 20, 1997

SEATTLE, Wash. – Tommie who?

After Nebraska's 27-14 victory over the second- and third-ranked Washington Huskies, there was no longer a question concerning the identity of the Nebraska quarterback. It was not Tommie Frazier. He'd been gone for two years. It was Scott Frost. Finally.

Of course, Frost's family and close friends would tell you that he'd been here all along, through the 11-2 season in 1996, the same old Frosty. But not until this day did Frost introduce himself as a quarterback who could lead Nebraska in a big game and maybe even to a national championship.

This was seen as the biggest game on Nebraska's 1997 calendar. For the Huskers, picturesque Husky Stadium, sitting on the edge of Lake Washington, was a proving field. Did the Huskers still have it as a national power?

The answer was a resounding yes, with all the trimmings. Nebraska bulled straight through and over the Washington defense, which ranked No. 1 in the nation against the rush. They opened big holes. They rushed for 384 yards. They knocked Husky quarterback Brock Huard out of the game early with an ankle injury. Before a hostile crowd dressed in purple-and-gold, they controlled everything.

And the man at the controls was Frost.

The native son, from Wood River, Neb., was finally able to shake off the trail of controversy that followed him: the transfer from Stanford, the Lawrence Phillips incident, the loss to Arizona State and replacing Frazier. It all came together for Frost in breathtaking fashion.

Nebraska fullback Joel Makovicka and I-back Ahman Green each rushed for 129 yards, but Frost blazed the biggest trails and drove the biggest nails. He ran 34 and 30 yards for touchdowns on Nebraska's first two series to stake NU to a 14-0 lead that set the dramatic tone of the day.

Frost vindicated the confidence bestowed upon him by coach Tom Osborne, who designed both touchdown plays for Frost. The first came with Frost moving Nebraska 80 yards in six plays and capping the drive himself on a quarterback delay that went off-tackle for 34 yards and a touchdown. The other was a quarterback draw that Frost ran to perfection that ended a 10-play, 56-yard drive with 1:51 left in the first quarter. Frost, in shotgun formation, took the snap, hesitated, eluded a Husky at the line of scrimmage, then shook two other defenders and raced untouched for the 30-yard score. The image of Frost streaking into the end zone twice on two possessions was a stunning sight, particularly to many Husker fans – some of whom had booed him the week before at home. But not Osborne.

"I thought he played great football today," Osborne said, "and he's doing as many things well as anyone we've had."

While Nebraska was flying on Frost's play-making and leadership, Washington was about to lose its leader. Junior Huard, the nation's top-rated passer after two games, suffered a sprained ankle when Husker senior rush end Grant Wistrom dived at his ankles and rolled on it. Huard left and freshman Marques Tuiasosopo came in. The freshman gave the Huskies a boost, leading them to a touchdown with 1:38 left in the half to cut the Huskers' lead to 21-7.

Tuiasosopo took Washington to another score in the third quarter and suddenly it was a seven-point game. But then came a huge gamble by Husky coach Jim Lambright. With 2:49 to go in the third quarter, he called for an onside kick "to get the momentum." The curious, calculated risk failed. Nebraska recovered. The Huskers then drove to a 20-yard field goal by Kris Brown for a 24-14 lead with 12:45 remaining. Washington never threatened again.

But now the Huskers had a new-found threat at quarterback. And their championship aura, after a sabattical, had returned.

"This victory gives us back that confidence that we had when we pretty much dominated college football in '94 and '95," said senior defensive tackle Jason Peter. "We feel we can play with anybody now."

When Washington quarterback Brock Huard went out with an early injury, the Huskers and Jason Wiltz (99) just went after quarterback Marques Tulasosopo.

Red Zone

The much-maligned Scott Frost takes time to revel in his finest moment as a Husker.

What didn't Grant Wistrom do against the Sooners? Here, the Lombardi Trophy winner knocks the ball loose from Oklahoma quarterback Brandon Daniels and later recovered the ball.

Red Zone Game 47

Nebraska 69, Oklahoma 7
Nov. 1, 1997

LINCOLN – It was ironic. And a little sad.

Nebraska coach Tom Osborne, in his 25th season, won his 250th career game, 69-7 over Oklahoma, on a day of fireworks – both on the field and in the dark early evening Nebraska sky following the game.

It was the most complete victory of the season thus far for the Huskers, who had 552 total yards and scored on 11 of their 15 possessions and led 34-0 at halftime. It was the worst loss in Oklahoma football history, which brings up the irony of the day. Osborne's milestone came against the school that had been his biggest nemesis and chief rival, especially early in his career when even he wondered if Oklahoma would ever let him get this far in his career.

Throw in the fact that this was the last game between the traditional rivals until the year 2000 – the Big 12 schedule necessitated a two-year break – and Thomas Lott, Billy Sims and Keith Jackson would have had to see it to believe it.

"We didn't want to let Coach Osborne down," Nebraska senior rush end Grant Wistrom said. "He'll be the first guy to downplay the significance of 250 wins and give credit to everyone else. We all know who got the program to this level and we'd give our heart and soul to the man. It would have been a shame to go out there and ruin his day."

There was no chance of that because Lott, Sims and Jackson were names in a record book. Nobody recognized Oklahoma anymore, especially Sooner fans. In coach John Blake's second year, the talent had slipped drastically and the Sooners were losing to most everyone. They couldn't run. They couldn't play defense. It was ugly. It was sad. They had lost seven straight to Nebraska and lost the last three in the series by 179-28. This wasn't a rivalry. It was cruelty.

That trend continued early and often on a strange Nov. 1 day that brought every form of weather imaginable to Lincoln. The constant was Oklahoma turnovers. Four Sooner fumbles led to 20 of Nebraska's first 27 points. Three of them were forced by Wistrom (who had 10 tackles, two sacks and a fumble recovery), who started the second quarter with a SportsCenter Highlight play, beating his man on the corner, stripping a Sooner of the ball and then recovering it himself. On the next play, NU quarterback Scott Frost hit freshman wingback Bobby Newcombe with a 40-yard touchdown strike to make it 27-0.

It was 55-0 by the time the Sooners scored, on a pass from Eric Moore to tight end Stephen Alexander with 2:05 left in the third quarter. So the Blackshirts couldn't give Osborne a shutout. Would he settle for a nice rainbow? An immaculate one rose up into the late afternoon sky in the fourth quarter, symoblic of the day. Soon, darkness fell and the Sooners jogged toward the locker room and everyone in a red jersey was wearing a special "Tom Osborne 250th victory" ball cap. A special ceremony, in which co-captain Jason Peter presented Osborne the game ball, took place. Osborne thanked everyone, passed the credit, and then bright fireworks sparkled in the sky. If there was any sadness, it was that the Oklahoma series was over, and wasn't the same anymore, anyway. But this was not a melancholy moment.

"To win 250 games in 25 years is unbelievable," Frost said. "I don't know if anyone will ever be able to do that again in college football. To be a part of that, to be on the field when he won his 250th, is definitely special to me."

The only way it could have been better is if Barry Switzer had to watch.

Red Zone

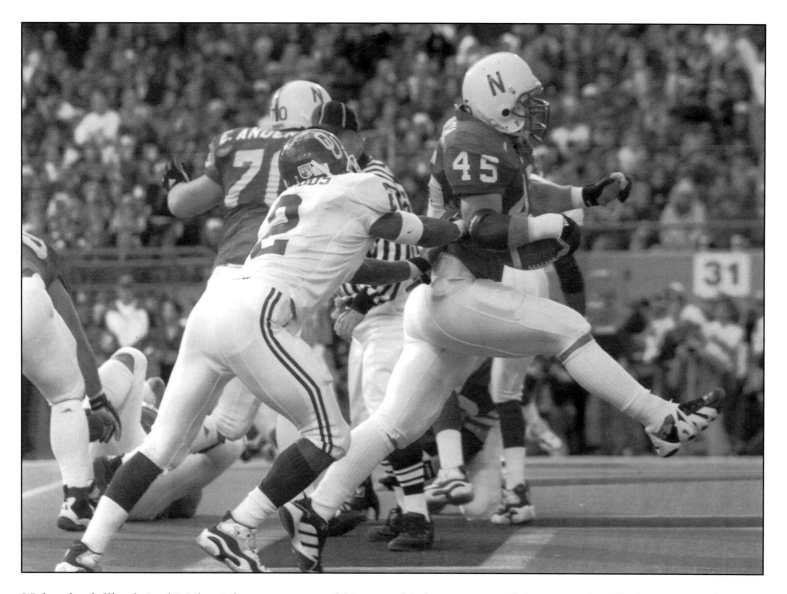

Nebraska fullback Joel Makovicka scores one of his two third-quarter touchdowns in the Huskers' rout of Oklahoma.

Nebraska freshman receiver Matt Davison holds up the ball seconds after he saved the catch, the season and the national championship.

Red Zone

Red Zone Game 48

Nebraska 45, Missouri 38 (OT)
Nov. 8, 1997

COLUMBIA, Mo. – Husker Magic.

That's the only explanation for what transpired at Faurot Field on Nov. 8, 1997. It was something Nebraska would never forget and something most of Nebraska never even saw, including the players on the field, except for the hundreds of replays that would be shown over the next several weeks.

"All I saw," said Nebraska quarterback Scott Frost, "was the brown thing bouncing around and the ref raised his hands."

The brown thing was the football, glorious and still air-born, from Frost's hands to the quick-thinking feet of wingback Shevin Wiggins to the ever-ready hands of freshman receiver Matt Davison in the Missouri end zone. The most improbable touchdown – and most improbable victory – in Nebraska history was good for an ESPY Award, a 45-38 overtime victory for the Huskers, a Big 12 Conference championship and Tom Osborne's third national championship, not necessarily in that order.

At the time the national title dream was in jeopardy. With Michigan thumping No. 2 Penn State that day, Nebraska's close call to 29-point underdog Mizzou helped drop the Huskers from No. 1 to No. 3 behind Michigan and Florida State. Many voters used Davison's miracle

catch as a reason to drop Nebraska. But, in the end, it kept their dream alive. They couldn't have won the coaches' national title without it.

Now, where were we?

Let's see. Huskers trail, 38-31. Seven seconds left. Frost throws a pass to Wiggins, who drops it while being hit, but still keeps the presence of mind to kick the ball up and keep it alive, perhaps for himself, but, better yet, for Davison, the true freshman who was so good he had to play this year and now we see why: Davison, who happened to be in the neighborhood, dove for the loose ball and just barely sneaked his two hands above the tallest strand of Missouri grass for the touchdown as time expired.

Sure.

That sounds like something Oklahoma ("Sooner Magic" they called it) used to do to Osborne in the final minute. Or Miami in the Orange Bowl. Or Florida State in the Orange Bowl. Were the football gods finally relenting on the I.O.U. to Osborne? Nobody was sure how it happened. And that included Davison.

"I saw the ball deflected off Shevin," Davison said. "It was floating like a punt, kind of end over end. It just seemed like it took forever to get there. I dove, and I guess the Lord was watching over me. I was in the right spot at the right time."

The greatest victory in Missouri history was on hold. Hundreds of pre-mature celebrating Tiger students had to be ushered away from a goalpost and back into the stands. There was overtime to be played.

Missouri won the toss and elected to play defense from its 25 (the new NCAA overtime system). Nebraska, recharged by Davison's play, scored in four plays with Frost diving over on an option play. But MU quarterback Corby Jones, who had played so brilliantly all game, couldn't answer. NU held on a three-yard run by Jones, two incompletions and finally a sack of Jones on fourth down by a pair of Missouri natives – rush ends Grant Wistrom and Mike Rucker. Game over. Dream on.

That was the only time the Huskers stopped Missouri and it was just in time. The Blackshirts looked lost and helpless, from MU's game-opening 12-play, 78-yard touchdown drive to its final score – a 15-yard touchdown pass from Jones to a wide-open Eddie Brooks. Jones, who passed for 233 yards, took full advantage of a young NU secondary and several breakdowns. His play-action passes made for a long, scary afternoon for Nebraska. Missouri, which led 24-21 at the half, seemed to score at will.

The Huskers didn't help their cause. Frost threw an interception inside the MU 11-yard line in the second quarter. Before halftime, with no timeouts, Frost let the play clock wind down and then bobbled a hurried shotgun snap and fell on the ball. End of half. No field goal.

In the third quarter, I-back Ahman Green lost a fumble deep in MU territory.

But Frost made up for it with a last-ditch drive that John Elway would be proud of. Taking over at his 33, with 62 seconds left and trailing 38-31, Frost led one of the great drives in Nebraska history. He completed four passes to move the Huskers from their 33 to the Missouri 12 with 14 seconds left. Frost spiked the ball to stop the clock. He threw incomplete on second down. Seven seconds left. Time for one more play.

The first look on the play was supposed to go to wingback Lance Brown in the left corner. But Frost saw that Brown couldn't have scored had he caught it. So he fired it over the middle to Wiggins. The rest, as they say, is history.

Husker Magic.

NU quarterback Scott Frost scores over Harold Piersey (2) in the first-quarter of the Huskers' classic at Missouri.

Missouri natives Mike Rucker (top) and Grant Wistrom (bottom) make a rush-end sandwich out of Tiger quarterback Corby Jones on fourth down in overtime and Nebraska had escaped.

Scott Frost stiff-arms Warrick Holdman of Texas A&M early in the Big 12 championship game in San Antonio.

Red Zone Game 49

Nebraska 54, Texas A&M 15
Dec. 6, 1997

SAN ANTONIO, Tx. – Finally, it was the Big Red Conference.

That's why Nebraska's 54-15 victory over Texas A&M was not only important, but one of the most significant victories of the decade. This was the Big 12 championship game in the Alamodome. This was Nebraska's first Big 12 football title.

Finally, Nebraska had proven its point to the new league. Or, 54 of them, to be exact.

This was more than about football. After two years of being outnumbered in Big 12 board rooms, the Huskers struck back. This was for all the 11-1 votes with NU as the lone wolf. This was for the league's founding fathers having the audacity to create a championship game and one more dadgum hurdle on the way to the national championship game. This was for 1996, when Nebraska was on its way to the Sugar Bowl to play for No. 1 until it fell over the hurdle in a stunning 37-27 loss to Texas – of all people – that prevented the Huskers from a fourth straight national title game.

It wasn't Texas, but Texas A&M on the River Walk was close enough.

"Our battle cry throughout summer workouts was that we always had a chip on our shoulders with what happened to us in St. Louis," said Nebraska senior rush end Grant Wistrom. "This is not redemption for us, but it definitely helps out and eases the pain a little bit. But that loss last year will stick with me forever."

Of course, because when the Big Eight and Southwest Conferences merged in 1995, Nebraska vs. Texas represented the battle of wits, cultures and power. Who would run the league? Too often, the "Texas" schools won in the board rooms. Now, it was time to settle it on the field.

This was settled early. The Huskers won in a River Walk. Even with the majority of the largest crowd to see a football game in the Alamodome – 64,824 – doing the Aggie Yell, and the Aggie band drowning out the Husker fans, Nebraska stormed the cadets early and often. It was 16-0 after one quarter, 37-3 at the half and by then Texas A&M coach R.C. Slocum was talking to his team "about pride."

The Huskers had stepped on that pride most of the half. Texas A&M, which had averaged 233 yards rushing per game, had a minus-five yards rushing at halftime. Texas A&M's first 14 plays, covering five possessions, netted all of three yards. At the half, the Aggies had 83 total yard, with 63 coming on one pass play. And this was with All-America defensive tackle Jason Peter out most of the half with a bad back.

With so few A&M possessions, that meant more for

Nebraska's offense and the Huskers used their time well. They rolled up 348 yards at the half, with quarterback Scott Frost throwing for 176 and a season-high 201 total yards. The other star was Ahman Green, the junior I-back who rushed for 179 yards and scored three touchdowns on runs of one, six and 25 yards – the latter coming with Green tip-toeing down the sideline and wiping out an official as he dived in. Green, who had a career-high 34 carries, moved his season total to 1,877 yards, the second-best one-season total in NU history behind Mike Rozier's total of 2,148 in 1983.

The Husker starters played well into the fourth quarter, but there was another point to prove. Nebraska was a solid No. 2 in both polls, behind Michigan, which had only to beat Washington State in the Rose Bowl to win at least one national title, if not two. The Huskers were trying to win back votes after losing some in a harried second-half victory at Colorado the previous week. The Aggies would pick up two touchdowns and 142 of their 277 total yards in the fourth quarter, but it wouldn't matter. Nebraska entered its Orange Bowl date with Tennessee at No. 2 and needed some help from Washington State, which is why Nebraska Athletic Director Bill Byrne wore a "Temporary Washington State Fan" shirt afterwards. But, if nothing else, the Huskers had accomplished one mission.

They had proved they were the best football program in the Big 12 and it wasn't as close as the score indicated.

Red Zone

Jason Peter didn't play long in the Big 12 game because of back spasms, but he made the most of his time. Here Peter celebrates a sack with Mike Rucker.

Tom Osborne runs onto the field for the last time as Nebraska head coach.

Red Zone

Red Zone Game 50

Nebraska 42, Tennessee 17
Jan. 2, 1998

MIAMI, Fla. – This time, with a national championship in the balance, Scott Frost was playing Bob Devaney.

The No. 2-ranked Huskers had just dispatched No. 3 Tennessee, 44-17, in the Orange Bowl but now came the hard part: waiting on the polls. No. 1 Michigan had beaten Washington State in the Rose Bowl the day before, 21-17, and the fear was that what the Huskers had done here might not have mattered.

So Frost couldn't wait. Much like Devaney, the former great Husker coach, had done before his first national title 18 years earlier in this same city, Frost tried to plant a last-ditch seed in the voters' minds.

"The AP (Associated Press poll) has pretty much given it away," said the senior Husker quarterback. "It's up to the coaches. I basically have two points for the coaches.

"One, if you can look yourself in the mirror and say if your job depended on playing either Michigan or Nebraska, who would you rather play?" The Rose Bowl ended with a controversial play. We took apart the third-ranked team in the country.

"Two, I can't see how any coach outside the Big Ten or Pac-10 could vote for Michigan. If the other coaches finished undefeated and won the Alliance Bowl game, they would expect to share the national title. It's been split before. It's OK to split it again."

Many reporters laughed. Frost's pleas came off more as honest, youthful emotion than a planned speech. The Huskers all wanted to win a share of the national championship for their coach, Tom Osborne, in his last game.

Osborne would not campaign. Not now, not ever. In 25 years as coach, that was never his style. He especially wanted to take the low-key approach to the Orange Bowl. But ever since he caught the world of college football off-guard by announcing his retirement from coaching back on Dec. 10, there was no chance for Osborne to slip quietly off into the south Florida sunset. Not with No. 1 at stake. The topic was broached at every press conference, around every corner. Osborne tried to treat it as just another game. But this was anything but just another game.

That was obvious the night of Jan. 2.

A crowd of 72,385 fans – half dressed in red, the other in orange – came to see who would have the best finale: Osborne or Volunteer quarterback Peyton Manning. It wasn't even close.

Well, maybe for a half. Nebraska led, 14-3, – mostly on Frost's passing – after 30 minutes. Many had questioned whether Tennessee, from the pass-happy "finesse" Southeastern Conference, could handle the Huskers' bru-

Nebraska quarterback Scott Frost was too much for Tennessee's Deon Grant on this third-quarter touchdown run in the 1998 Orange Bowl.

Red Zone

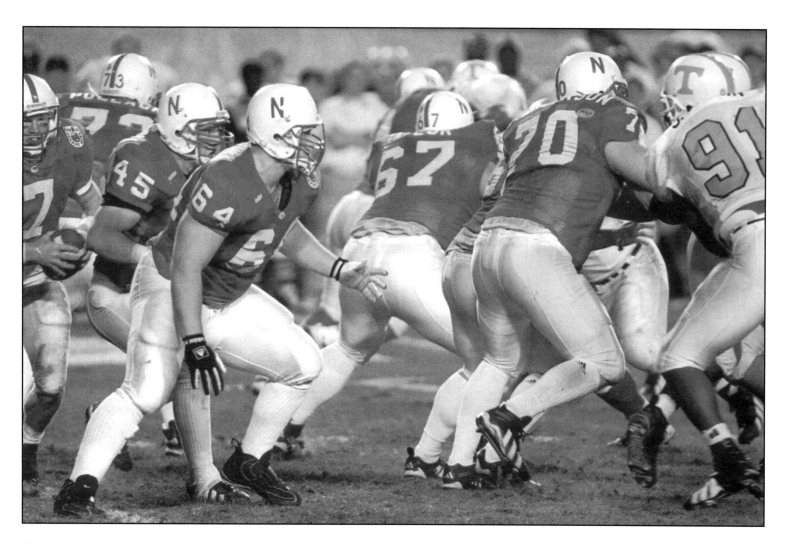

Scott Frost and the Husker offense was on a mission against Tennessee in the Orange Bowl: win a national championship for Tom Osborne in his final game.

tal running game. But the Vols did just fine, holding NU to seven yards in the first two possessions, and had to feel good being so close despite two Tennessee turnovers. The only problem was Manning, who was playing on a painful knee injury, could never get untracked. The injury had limited his mobility. He couldn't roll out or take a seven-step drop because of the risk of the NU pass rush doing further damage.

Not that it would have mattered.

Osborne could take pride in knowing his last game was pure T.O. The coach famous for his halftime adjustments had a doozy: in an uncharacteristic emotional speech, Osborne told the Huskers to "keep putting points on the board and keep pounding them."

Nebraska responded by burying the Vols in a three-touchdown third quarter so typical of Osborne's career. The offensive line kicked in. And junior I-back Ahman Green, who rushed for an Orange Bowl record 206 yards, rode the wave.

Green rushed 13 times for 159 yards – with runs of 14, 43, 47 and 22 – and one touchdown in the quarter. The Huskers started smashing mouths, opening holes, owning the trenches. They ran off scoring drives of 80 yards in 12 plays, 73 yards in six plays, both ending in Frost touchdown runs, and 80 yards in four plays with Green going the final 22 yards. That made it 35-10.

Manning, who completed a great college career by com-pleting 21-of-31 passes for 134 yards, suffered the same fate of many Husker opposing quarterbacks: He was kept on the sidelines by the Nebraska rushing machine.

Meanwhile, as Frost scored late in the fourth quarter to try and pad NU's poll resume, the tension mounted on the Husker sideline. Osborne was still stone-faced and into the game when co-captains Jason Peter and Grant Wistrom ambushed him with a Gatorade bath. All Osborne could do was smile.

The clock ticked down. Nebraska fans started chanting "T.O.! T.O.! T.O.!" What an unforgettable scene, an incredible way for Osborne to leave the bowl that had defined his resilient career and leave the game and players he loved. Then, from the trophy presentation to the CBS interview to the press conference, the questions came: What about No. 1? Did you do enough, Tom?

"We've done all we can," Osborne said, in a statement that was pure Osborne and summarized his career, too.

Later, as he put on his pajamas and packed suitcases with family and friends back in his Sheraton Bal Harbour room on Miami Beach, the news came across ESPN about 2 a.m.: The coaches had voted Nebraska No. 1 by a small margin.

Tom Osborne, who always said it was the journey and not the destination that mattered, could now pack a happy ending into his suitcase. The journey was finally over.

Red Zone

Great Losses

Miami (Fla.) 31, Nebraska 30
Jan. 2, 1984

MIAMI, Fla. – Most losses hurt. And then there are those rarest of defeats, the ones that make you feel good and even proud to be associated with a school, a game and a group of young men.

Nebraska's 31-30 loss to Miami in the 1984 Orange Bowl was such a defeat.

The events that transpired on the Orange Bowl Stadium turf that night have been called one of the greatest, and certainly one of the most unforgettable, games ever. And all because of a no-brainer, no-hesitation, no-nonsense, all-guts decision made by Nebraska head coach Tom Osborne at the climax.

Nebraska had just scored a touchdown. And now, with 48 seconds left, and his No.-1 ranked Huskers trailing "home team" Miami, 31-30, Osborne could have kicked the extra point and forged a tie that no doubt would have meant at least a share of the national championship – his first national title. His team had been ranked at the top all season and had mowed through the competition at record paces. They had to play their bowl on their opponent's home field. And No. 2 Texas and No. 3 Michigan had lost that day. Kick?

Osborne went for two – and the victory.

And lost.

Turner Gill's pass attempt to I-back Jeff Smith in the end zone was tipped and broken up by Miami safety Ken Calhoun. The frenzied Orange Bowl crowd exploded in joy. Back home, Nebraskans wept. But through the tears, they could feel warm and proud. Their coach had done the right thing.

And now the nation knew. For so long, the image of Osborne was of a quiet, religious man who produced winning teams but couldn't beat Oklahoma. He didn't have what it took to win a national title. But now the whole country knew that Osborne had more than what it takes to be a champion. Osborne's decision suddenly defined him and his career. It made him human to a generation of football fans. He was gutsy. A leader. A hero.

"We were trying to win the game," Osborne said. "I don't think you go for a tie in that case. You try to win the game. We wanted an undefeated season and a clear-cut national championship."

Osborne knew that wasn't going to be easy, even with his 13-0 Huskers, who included the 1983 Heisman Trophy winner in Mike Rozier and Outland and Lombardi winner in tackle Dean Steinkuhler. Miami was talented and on a roll. And Hurricane coach Howard Schnellenberger had worked south Florida into a pre-game frenzy.

It worked. Miami, with sophomore quarterback Bernie Kosar's unorthodox style, blitzed the Huskers for a 17-0 lead. The Huskers were on their heels. They had attempted to confuse Kosar before the game when cornerback Dave Burke and strong safety Mike McCashland switched jerseys. But the move only underscored NU's lack of confidence against Kosar. Then, when the Huskers resorted to the "fumblerooski" – with Steinkuhler picking up the snap and scoring – it made NU look desperate. But the Huskers had rarely been pushed all season, especially with a three- and four-receiver offense like Miami's, with a quarterback as hot as Kosar and in front of a crowd this wild.

The Huskers regrouped, tieing the game at 17 on Scott Livingston's 35-yard field goal with 13:09 left in the third quarter. But Kosar again threw passes to put the 'Canes ahead, 31-17. Worse, Rozier had left the game with a sprained ankle.

His replacement, Smith, was thrust into the spotlight and responded with 99 yards on nine carries. The junior fumbled at the Miami two-yard line after a 35-yard run in the third quarter, but he came back to pull NU within one, 31-30, with a 24-yard touchdown run.

And then came the defining moment – for Osborne, and Nebraska.

"There was no doubt in Tom Osborne's mind, and there was no doubt in my mind," Schnellenberger said. "It was a championship game, and he went after it like a champion."

Miami would be voted No. 1. But in the hearts and minds of those who saw this game, Osborne and Nebraska were champions.

Great Losses

Florida State 18, Nebraska 16
Jan. 1, 1994

MIAMI, Fla.– He was at peace. That's the first thing you noticed about Tom Osborne on the morning after.

It was about 7 a.m. The Nebraska football coach was poolside out back of the Huskers' Miami Beach hotel, the Sheraton Bal Harbour. He was taping his TV show, just several hours after one of the wildest rides any Nebraska fan had ever taken. And though the ride ended in a stunning, controversial 18-16 defeat to Florida State in another Orange Bowl for the national championship, the serene look on Osborne's face gave you the feeling the Biggest Red could live with this one.

He could handle the bitter disappointment of Husker kicker Byron Bennett's last-second kick going wide left. He could stomach the call that should have been made and one that shouldn't. He could deal with coming up short on another national title attempt – in the same dadgummed stadium and same end zone, to boot.

Osborne could live with it because his Huskers, who had been 17 1/2-point underdogs, had outplayed No. 1-ranked Florida State. In fact, the Seminoles had to win it twice. And nobody was sure then if they had won it, or even deserved to.

"This hurts," Osborne said, "But it's a different kind of hurt. I told my team I was proud of them. People play for rings and trophies, but as far as I'm concerned we won.

We didn't win on the scoreboard, but we played great football. The main thing isn't the rings and the championships. It's playing like champions, and that's what we did."

It had been a while for the Huskers, who finshed 11-1 in 1993. They finished ranked third behind FSU (12-1) and Notre Dame (11-1) but it was their first top-10 finish in five seasons. The college football world had forgotten Nebraska was a threat.

The Huskers proved they belonged again behind classic performances by sophomore quarterback Tommie Frazier and senior rush end Trev Alberts, who evoked the most memorable images of this wild, wild night. Alberts led a Blackshirt defense that sacked FSU quarterback Charlie Ward five times (the 1993 Heisman Trophy winner had been sacked only 10 times all season) and harrassed and confused the Seminole scoring machine all night. Frazier outplayed Ward. But he couldn't overcome the officiating.

This game will burn in Nebraska memories for two calls. The first came during Corey Dixon's electric 71-yard touchdown on a punt return in the first quarter – one that was called back on a clipping penalty that replays could never pinpoint. The other came in the third quarter, with FSU at the Nebraska goalline, when fullback William Floyd was hit by the Husker roverback Toby

Wright as he crossed the goalline. This time, TV replays showed the ball was loose before it crossed the plane. But FSU was given a touchdown and 12-7 lead.

It was 15-7 when Frazier started the comeback. He completed passes of 15 and 26 yards to Dixon between a 16-yard run by freshman Lawrence Phillips, who finished the drive with a 12-yard touchdown run. A two-point conversion try by Frazier failed, but NU had cut the FSU lead to 15-13 on the first play of the fourth quarter.

Then, with 4:39 left, Frazier drove the Huskers from their 20 to the FSU nine-yard line. The drive stalled and Bennett came on to kick a 27-yard field goal. With 1:16 left to play, Nebraska led, 16-15.

But then Ward began to show his Heisman form. He had help. Nebraska shot itself in the foot continually, starting with the kickoff that went out of bounds and set up FSU at its 35. The Huskers offered up two back-breaking penalties: a late hit and a pass interference call that put the Seminoles to the Nebraska three-yard line. The drive took all of 55 seconds.

On third down, FSU coach Bobby Bowden decided not to tempt the football gods that had crushed him time and again in his career. He sent freshman kicker Scott Bentley in to make a 22-yard field goal. Bentley made it. With 21 seconds left, FSU began celebrating Bowden's first title.

Not so fast. Frazier wasn't done. After FSU was penalized 15 yards for excessive celebration, and one incomplete pass, Frazier hit tight end Trumane Bell with a 29-yard pass to the FSU 28. But the clock kept ticking ... .0:02 ... 0:01 ... Frazier was hurrying his offense ... and finally 0:00. FSU players stormed the field. But wait. The officials ruled that one second was still remaining. Bowden, wet from a Gatorade shower, had to usher his team off the field for Bennett's 27-yard field goal attempt.

He missed. Finally, FSU could celebrate. Finally, Bowden had won his national title. And finally, Nebraska was back. Because most everyone knew the better team had not won.

"I guess it was our time," Bowden said, "because Nebraska played as good or better than we did. Nebraska is a lot better than I thought. A lot better."

Red Zone

Frank Solich Profile

Frank Solich is now the big man on campus.

OK, enough size jokes already. Solich, who will lead Nebraska football into the next era and century, has dealt with the size cracks since coming to Nebraska in 1962 as a 5-foot-8, 157-pound fullback out of Cleveland's Holy Name High School.

The Nebraska media guide referred to him as "probably the smallest major-college fullback in the country." He also had the honor of making Sports Illustrated, which referred to him as "the size of an underdeveloped cheerleader."

His own Nebraska coach, Bob Devaney, once said, "Frank Solich was quite a football player for his size." Of course, Devaney then added, "In fact, he was quite a football player, period."

Beginning in the fall of 1998, the world would see what kind of head coach Solich would become. Solich took the Big Red baton from Tom Osborne on Dec. 10, 1997. All of which surprised no one in Nebraska. Solich had long been rumored as Osborne's successor. He was seen as the perfect man to keep the Devaney-Osborne train on track. Solich may have been born in a western Pennsylvania coal-mining town and grown up in Cleveland, but he is red through-and-through.

For one, Solich was in Devaney's first recruiting class in Nebraska and later starred at fullback, where, in a game at Air Force in 1965, he rushed for 204 yards (and three touchdowns), a single-game Nebraska record that held up until 1976. After high-school coaching stints at Omaha's Holy Name High and Lincoln Southeast High (where he won two state titles), Solich joined Osborne's staff in 1979 as freshman coach and later was promoted to running backs coach and assistant head coach.

The latter promotion came in 1991, after Solich had turned an offer to join his former NU teammate, Wisconsin head coach Barry Alvarez, in Madison, Wis. Still, Solich wanted to run his own program. He was in the running for the Minnesota job in 1996 until KU's Glen Mason got the job in the 11th hour.

Would Solich ever get his chance? It came in 1997 when Osborne, concerned about his health and looking for a break, also remembered a commitment he had made to Solich to pass the baton to him one day. Solich, who took the job at 53, wasn't getting any younger. So Osborne stepped aside, but only with the assurance Solich would get the job. Thus, Osborne had hand-picked Solich much like Devaney had chosen Osborne.

Will the formula continue to work its time-tested charm? Solich knows the Nebraska system well. He's vowed to not change a thing, though he's smart enough – as both Devaney and Osborne were – to tinker along with the times. He benefited from having the entire coaching staff stay on to see him through a smooth transition his first year. And Osborne has left him a cupboard full of speed and size and an electrifying sophomore quarterback in Bobby Newcombe.

But continuing to feed the monster won't be easy. It wasn't for Osborne in 1973 and that was before scholarship cuts and Title IX demands on the budget. The national championship system, too, has changed: in the Bowl Championship Series format, a computer ranking based on strength of schedule will count greatly toward who plays in the national title game. Solich will have to weigh that against the financial demands for home games.

It should be most interesting. But Solich might be the perfect mix. He is part-Devaney: while filling in for Osborne at the 1997 Big 12 Conference media day, Solich was the only coach to attend the media social functions. He is part-Osborne: quiet, reserved in his manner. Solich wouldn't move into Osborne's office until two months after Osborne was gone.

He also has a sense of humor, which will come in handy. During his introductory news conference, Solich laughed when senior Vershawn Jackson talked about the difference between Solich and Osborne.

"When you say a dropoff from Coach Osborne to Coach Solich, probably the biggest dropoff would be, you know.....look at Coach Osborne," Jackson said, pointing to the difference in height.

Suffice it to say Solich has a very large task at hand.

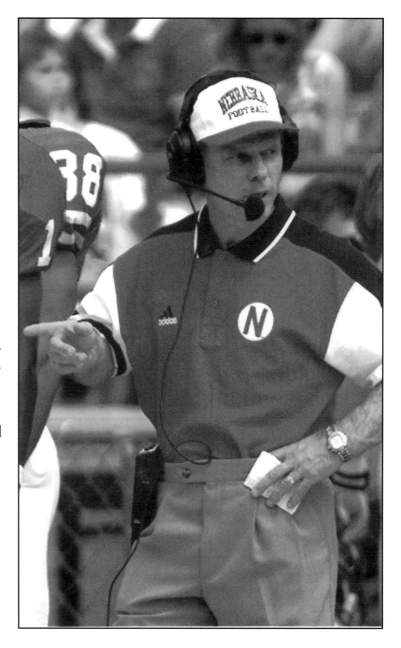

Red Zone